A STUDENT'S GUIDE TO COMMUNICATION AND SELF-PRESENTATION

Recommendations, Relationships, Résumés, and Interviews

Monica Reinhard-Gorney and Perk Musacchio

cognella® | ACADEMIC PUBLISHING

Bassim Hamadeh, CEO and Publisher

Kassie Graves, Acquisitions Editor

Berenice Quirino, Associate Production Editor

Miguel Macias, Senior Graphic Designer

Alexa Lucido, Licensing Associate

Don Kesner, Interior Designer

Natalie Piccotti, Senior Marketing Manager

Kassie Graves, Director of Acquisitions and Sales

Jamie Giganti, Senior Managing Editor

Cover image copyright © 2017 iStockphoto LP/Jacob Ammentorp Lund.

Printed in the United States of America

ISBN: 978-1-5165-1828-9 (pbk)

A STUDENT'S GUIDE TO COMMUNICATION AND SELF-PRESENTATION

Recommendations, Relationships, Résumés, and Interviews

DEDICATION

Monica:

To my husband, Robert Gorney Jr., my children, Ava and Cora Gorney, and my parents, Erna Reinhard and Fred Reinhard, who always emphasize the value of investing in an education, and to my early mentors in the field of education: Sally Goebel, Nancy Christy, and Georgia Bennett.

Perk:

To my high school English teacher, valued mentor, and professor at Temple University, Joseph Haviland, who will always be a favorite teacher and inspiration, and to Santa Mazolla who inspired me to become a special education teacher and diagnostician.

Together:

We would also like to express our sincere gratitude to Karen Dickinson and Rick Parsons for extending an invitation to contribute to this series and for their continued support with our endeavors. We would also like to thank Kassie Graves who listened to our "pitch" and helped turn it into a reality!

THE COGNELLA SERIES ON STUDENT SUCCESS

S tudent success isn't always measured in straight As.

Many students arrive at college believing that if they study hard and earn top grades, their higher education experience will be a success. Few recognize that some of their greatest learning opportunities will take place outside the classroom. Learning how to manage stress, navigate new relationships, or put together a budget can be just as important as acing a pop quiz.

The Cognella Series on Student Success is a collection of books designed to help students develop the essential life and learning skills needed to support a happy, healthy, and productive higher education experience. Featuring topics suggested by students and books written by experts, the series offers research-based, yet practical advice to help any student navigate new challenges and succeed throughout their college experience.

Series Editor: Richard Parsons, Ph.D.
Professor of Counselor Education, West Chester University

Other titles available in the series:

- *A Student's Guide to Stress Management*
- *A Student's Guide to a Meaningful Career*
- *A Student's Guide to College Transition*
- *A Student's Guide to Money Matters*
- *A Student's Guide to Self-Care*
- *A Student's Guide to Exercise for Improving Health*

ABOUT THE AUTHORS

No matter how skilled you may be in your area of study, interpersonal skills and the way in which you present yourself to those around you are paramount to your success.

A Student's Guide to Communication and Self-Presentation: Recommendations, Relationships, Résumés, and Interviews is designed to help you develop the communication, interpersonal, and self-presentation skills required to successfully interact with instructors and peers during your academic career, and managers, colleagues, and teams in your post-graduate, working life. The guide will help you navigate day-to-day interactions, prepare for interviews, cultivate emotional intelligence, and more.

With numerous opportunities for participation and reflection, this book encourages you to examine your current communication and self-presentation skills in an effort to improve upon them and, ultimately, set yourself apart from the crowd.

A Student's Guide to Communication and Self-Presentation is part of the Cognella Series on Student Success, a collection of books designed to help students develop the essential life and learning skills needed to support a happy, healthy, and productive higher education experience.

Monica Reinhard-Gorney is a certified school counselor and has 18 years of experience working with high school students in private and public settings. She has worked with students individually and in seminar settings, helping them prepare for undergraduate and graduate school admissions. She has an undergraduate degree from Bryn Mawr College and a master's degree from the University of Pennsylvania.

Perk Musacchio is a retired elementary and special education teacher and has over 40 years of experience in the world of education. After retirement, Perk started Skills2Soar, LLC, an educational consulting company. She earned her undergraduate degree from West Chester University and her master's degree from Temple University.

CONTENTS

EDITOR'S PREFACE

T he transition to college marks a significant milestone in a person's life. Many of you will be preparing to live away from your friends and family for the very first time. Clearly, this is and should be, an exciting time.

It is a time to experience new things and experiment with new options. While the opportunity to grow is clear—so too are the many challenges you are to experience as you transition from high school to college.

Research suggests that the first year of college is the most difficult period of adjustment a student faces. Not only will you be required to adjust to new academic demands but you will also have to navigate a number of social and emotional challenges that accompany your life as a college student. The books found within this series—*Cognella Series on Student Sucess*—have been developed to help you with the many issues confronting your successful transition from life as a high school student to life as a collegiate. Each book within the series was designed to provide research-based, yet *practical* advice to assist you succeeding in your college experience.

The current book, *A Student's Guide to Communication and Self-Presentation,* provides you with well-researched, practical advice in developing skills essential to presenting your thoughts, your ideas, your positions, and yourself in the best light possible.

The authors provide tips and strategies about communication and related skill sets that are designed to help you be successful in high school, during college or post–high school training, and up through your entry into the job market.

As you will soon come to discover, while the topic is serious, the manner in which the information is presented is both engaging and directly applicable to your own current life experience. The book employs case illustrations in a feature called "*Voices From Campus,*" and opportunities to apply what you are learning to your own life in a feature called "*Your Turn.*" I know that you will find this, as well as the other books within the series, to be a useful guide to your successful transition from high school to college.

Richard Parsons, Ph.D.
Series Editor

AUTHORS' PREFACE

A *Student's Guide to Communication and Self-Presentation* is a significant tool and reference guide for students as they journey through high school, then transition into college or post-secondary training, and all the way up through entry into the job market. Much is being written about the rate of unemployment and debt among recent college graduates. Government statistics show that college graduates account for over half of the unemployed population. Much of the literature written on this topic attributes this lack of employment, or the inability to retain employment, to weak communication and interpersonal skills. Our goal is to arm students with strong skills in the area of communication and self-presentation so that they have the best possible chance of success in both personal and professional relationships, as well as in the job market. This book requires the reader to be reflective and self-evaluative in order to grow. It is a journey that we hope will lead to great personal reward.

MRG/PM

ACKNOWLEDGMENTS

We have been blessed with friends, family, and colleagues who have also contributed their support and wealth of experiences and suggestions to this guide. We hope that they will be happy with the final product and know that their contributions will help many future high school and college students find their path to success and happiness. To all of you, please accept our appreciation and gratitude for your help with and support of this guide.

Harsimran S Baweja P.T. Ph.D., Assistant Professor, Physical Therapy and Applied Movement Sciences, College of Health and Human Services, San Diego State University, San Diego
Clif Beaver, Principal, Unionville-Chadds Ford School District
Linda Brodeur-Cangi, School Social Worker
Steven J. Capolarello, Adjunct Professor of Economics, West Chester University
James Chok, Ph.D., Clinical Neuropsychologist, Board Certified Behavior Analyst
Dave Filano, Wawa Inc., Manager of Talent Acquisition & Diversity
Sujit Joseph, Banker
Suzanne Kaplan, Millennial Decoder, President of Talent Balance, Consultant to TheRoadmap.com
Dave Musacchio, Sales Manager

Mike Musacchio, Sales Operations Manager
Steve Musacchio, Strength and Conditioning Coach
Tony Musacchio, Retired Educator
Karin Napier, VP Sales
Greg Newell, President of Nave Newell, Inc.
Thomas Sterner, friend, author of *The Practicing Mind*
Charles W. Thompson, Business Executive

CHAPTER 1

THE IMPORTANCE OF COMMUNICATION AND SELF-PRESENTATION SKILLS

"**W**hy Communication is Today's Most Important Skill"—a powerful headline and a topic recently featured in *Forbes Magazine*. The author, Greg Satell, highlights that one of the greatest leaders of all time, Winston Churchill, is remembered most for being an effective communicator. He goes on to share that the future belongs to innovators and that, "In order to innovate, it's not enough to just come up with big ideas, you also need to work hard to communicate them clearly."[i]

These thoughts are echoed in another article highlighted in *Forbes*, "7 Top VCs [Venture Capitalists] Say These Communication Skills Will Set You Apart." Michael Moritz, an investor behind Google, PayPal, Airbnb, and LinkedIn, says, "You cannot lead an individual—let alone a team or an organization—without being able to clearly communicate the direction in which you want to go." Bill Gurley of Benchmark Capital (behind Uber, Grubhub, and OpenTable) says that venture capitalists evaluate whether to invest based on "how well an entrepreneur can communicate his or her ideas."[ii]

[i] Satell, G. "Why Communication Is Today's Most Important Skill." *Forbes*. 6 Febuary 2015. Web. https://www.forbes.com/sites/gregsatell/2015/02/06/why-communication-is-todays-most-important-skill/#1566640c1100
[ii] Gallo, C. "Top 7 VCs Say These Communication Skills Will Set You Apart." *Forbes*. 28 March 2017. Web. https://www.forbes.com/sites/carminegallo/2017/03/28/7-top-vcs-say-these-communication-skills-will-set-you-apart/#46a502cb65df

The Career section of *U.S. News & World Report* recently featured, "4 Communications Skills to Highlight on Your Résumé." Arnie Fertig, the article's author, states, "It's hard to imagine any job that doesn't require you to communicate well!" He also shares some powerful words of wisdom, "You can demonstrate your communications skills when you speak of facilitating meetings, problem solving, marketing, and a host of other common workplace activities. The point is simple: Show your skills rather than simply claiming them. When you do, you will prove that indeed you are an excellent communicator."[iii]

One thing seems clear. Having good communication skills is important, and it is highly valued in the workforce. For some, having good communication skills comes naturally, but for many, having good communication skills requires focused attention. The good news is that most students, given proper instruction and practice, can improve their communication skills. Think of it this way, working to improve your communication skills is an investment in your personal and professional relationships and your future!

1.1: So What Are Communication and Self-Presentation?

Communication and self-presentation—huge words with significant meanings! What do they mean, and why are they relevant and important words for high school and college students to understand?

The Merriam-Webster dictionary defines communication as "the act or process of using words, sounds, signs, or behaviors to express or exchange information or to express your ideas, thoughts, feelings, etc., to someone else."[iv]

Communicating involves both sharing and receiving ideas and information. It is a two-way street and an important one!

1.2: Communication in the Academic Arena

The ability to communicate your thoughts and ideas verbally and in writing becomes an increasingly important skill as you grow older. In high school, with

iii Fertig, A. "4 Communication Skills to Highlight on Your Résumé." *U.S. News & World Report.* 6 October 2015. Web. http://money.usnews.com/money/blogs/outside-voices-careers/2015/10/06/4-communications-skills-to-highlight-on-your-resume

iv Communication [for English Language Learners], in *Merriam-Webster Online.* Web. https://www.merriam-webster.com/dictionary/communication https://www.merriam-webster.com/dictionary/communication

the exception of math courses, much of your grade can be based on written papers and/or presentations in class. In college, this continues to be the case.

Teachers and college professors are looking to see if you can do the following:

- Can you understand directions given verbally or in writing?
- Do your written papers stay on topic and follow the rubric, if one is provided?
- Is your writing clear and easy for the reader to understand?

1.3: Communication in the Social Arena

The ability to convey your thoughts, feelings, and ideas takes on equal importance in the classroom. Being able to respectfully listen to and consider the thoughts, feelings, and ideas of others usually leads to open and successful discussions, provided the other listeners are also able to do the same.

Teachers and college professors are looking to see if you can do the following:

- Can you communicate your thoughts and ideas effectively in class discussions?
- Can you listen to and interpret the thoughts, ideas, and feelings of others?
- Do you stay on topic in your presentations and convey your thoughts and ideas in a way that your audience understands?

The need for good communication skills extends beyond the classroom environment. We use communication skills in all our relationships, from those within our family, to our friendships, to our relationships with peers and teachers, and eventually, if you go on to college, with roommates and professors. When you enter a work environment, having good communication skills with co-workers and supervisors is critical. Good communication skills can lead to rewarding and successful relationships. However, oftentimes strained or bad relationships are a result of miscommunications and misunderstandings. One thing seems certain—having an awareness of how one communicates is an important life skill!

1.4: What Is Self-Presentation All About?

The definition of self-presentation is a little less clear-cut because it isn't actually a word in the dictionary; it is more of a "man-made" concept. The Babylon Thesaurus offers "impression management" as a synonym for self-presentation, and in many ways, that synonym perfectly captures the concept being discussed here.[v] Think of self-presentation as a conscious process in which you attempt to influence (or at least have an awareness of) the perceptions that others have of you.

VOICES FROM CAMPUS 1.1

The disappointing grade....

I recently turned in a paper in my Communications 101 class. I was super pumped up about it because I really enjoyed writing it and thought for sure I was going to receive an "A" as my grade. When my teacher returned the papers this week, I was super shocked to see a "C" written at the top. After looking at her comments, I realized that I had not addressed each aspect of the writing assignment the teacher had given. I had gotten really excited about a particular aspect of the paper that was personally meaningful to me, and I kind of went off on a tangent about it and forgot to address three other key points she had listed on the rubric. What a lesson learned. Had I remembered to look at the rubric when I thought I was done, I would have realized that I hadn't addressed all the points, and I could have gotten a better grade. I'll be sure to do that next time!

Self-presentation requires you to be aware of how you are being perceived and to potentially make adjustments if you are not being received the way you had hoped. This is not as easy as it sounds. First, you must decide that being received well matters. Then you have to be able to read the response of others. Responses come in verbal and nonverbal forms. Some people may directly tell you how they are feeling in response to what you have said or done, or they may indirectly send "signals" via body language. It is important to look for and understand these different forms of communication!

[v] Self-presentation, in *Babylon Thesaurus*. Web. http://thesaurus.babylon-software.com/self-presentation

1.5: A New Form of Communication

You, as high school or college students, are in the very unique position of being among the first generation that was raised with a form of communication that did not exist for many of the people you will interact with in your lifetime—a form of communication that is of a virtual nature and came with the creation of the Internet. The Internet led to other forms of communication that could be carried out through email and the many other forms of social media. While in the past, students only had to think about how they conveyed information via the spoken or written word, now thoughts, words, ideas, and much more can be shared over social media in the form of tweets, Facebook posts, YouTube videos, and more.

A strong argument can be made for how this additional form of communication has improved the world, some of which include:

- Information and ideas can be shared with ease around the world. Before, only a small number of people had the opportunity to share information, such as newsprint or TV reporters, magazine editors, etc.

- Students in classrooms in one location can interact with and learn from students in classrooms across the globe using Skype or other forms of video conferencing.

- All people have the opportunity to create a platform, giving lots of people opportunities and a voice, especially increasing opportunities for people to share ideas and talents that might not have been discovered without the Internet.

- Friendships and familial relationships can be maintained at a distance with ease.

- There are now undergraduate and graduate degrees that can be earned by participating in classes online or via video conferencing.

- Co-workers can interact with other co-workers in different offices, cutting down on travel expenses for many companies.

An equally strong argument can be made for some of the challenges that have come with the virtual world, some of which include:

- Children can easily access information that could once be guarded more closely by adults.

- People of all ages can share whatever information they want to, which can include sharing video and photos of others without their permission.

- Any and all information, even information that is false or misleading, can be put out there and then easily seen.

- People can share their thoughts and feelings instantaneously and with a large audience. Sometimes words and messages are conveyed with little thought, and once they are out there, they cannot just be taken back.

- People can put their conflicts out there for all to see. Before the Internet, people tended to resolve conflicts between themselves, either in person or in the written form, with few people involved. Of course, gossip and lies were spread back before the Internet, but now damage to people and reputations can be done on a large scale and at a global level rather than on a small scale.

VOICES FROM CAMPUS 1.2

It's Best To Think Things Through....

When I got to school on Monday morning, I was called into the guidance office. I couldn't imagine why because I hadn't requested to see my counselor. When she called me in, I was shocked that the assistant principal was sitting in the room with her. I was really feeling nervous now. They proceeded to tell me that a video had been brought to their attention. Over the weekend I had been hanging out with friends, and we were just being goofy, but we made a video that was making fun of a few of our classmates. I was horrified to hear that most of the teachers in the school had seen it. I was beyond embarrassed and now worried what my teachers were going to think of me. I hadn't meant any harm by it, but now in hindsight, I realize that it had hurt a number of my classmates. I just thought I was having fun with my friends. I never thought about the fact that the video could get out there. It turns out one of my friends sent a copy of the video to one of her friends, and she is the one who posted it on the Internet. I feel like people are going to think differently about me now. I wish I had thought all this through before making that video.

Why students have to be aware of the virtual world today:

- Many have found themselves on the receiving end of Internet attacks, hoaxes, or predators.

- The messages shared on apps such as Twitter, Facebook, and SnapChat can now potentially be viewed by friends, parents, teachers, college admissions officers, and future employers. Some of those viewers may have issues with content shared, so having good control of one's Internet presence is important.

- Though students have a comfort level with using the virtual world, not everyone else in the world does, which could lead to differences and issues in communication styles with teachers, professors, co-workers, and future job supervisors.

1.6: Real World Communication, Self-Presentation

A story made major news headlines in the spring of 2016. The NFL draft was soon to take place and a young man named Laremy Tunsil had been receiving lots of press because he was expected to be an early round pick. However, 13 minutes before the draft began, a video was posted to his Twitter account that showed him wearing a gas mask and appearing to be inhaling a drug through a bong. Word spread instantly at the draft. Teams that had spoken to the press about wanting to pick him up became concerned about Tunsil's decision making. He was expected to be pick number six going to the Baltimore Ravens (some even estimated he'd go as the third pick). However, he ended up being pick number 13, going to the Miami Dolphins. *Fortune Magazine*, in an article entitled, "Here's How Much NFL Draft Pick Laremy Tunsil Lost Because of 1 Tweet," estimates that this video cost Tunsil eight million in salary.[vi]

No doubt Laremy Tunsil learned an important and costly lesson. And in fact, he used his self-presentation skills to attempt to begin to repair his public image by addressing the matter head on during his interviews following the draft. He shared that his Twitter account had been hacked, that the video had been taken years ago, and that it did not represent who he was now. When asked repeatedly if he was disappointed in the draft

vi Chew, J. "Here's How Much NFL Draft Pick Laremy Tunsil Lost Because of 1 Tweet." *Fortune.* 29 April 2016. Web. http://fortune.com/2016/04/29/laremy-tunsil-tweet-video/

outcome, rather than say that he was disappointed he had gone thirteenth instead of third, he said that he was truly grateful to be a part of the draft at all and to have been selected by the Dolphins. He promised to work as hard as he could and to make his family, teammates, and the Dolphin's organization proud.

And then there was the 2017 situation that caused Harvard College to rescind admissions offers to at least 10 prospective members of the Class of 2021. Since many of you reading this book may currently or soon be applying to college, pay close attention! It turns out some admitted students had set up a private Facebook group chat, and it had come to the attention of the Harvard Admissions office, who then released the following statement in part, "The Admissions Committee was disappointed to learn that several students in a private group chat for the Class of 2021 were sending messages that contained offensive messages and graphics." The description for the official Facebook group for the Class of 2021, set up and maintained by the Admissions Office, disclaims all administrative responsibility for "unofficial groups." The email went on to warn admitted students that their admissions offers could be rescinded under specific circumstances. "As a reminder, Harvard College reserves the right to withdraw an offer of admission under various conditions including if an admitted student engages in behavior that brings into question his or her honesty, maturity, or moral character."[vii] Imagine what the future could have looked like for those students with a diploma from Harvard. Now, those students must accept the consequences for their poor judgment and inappropriate use of social media and fall back on what other options they might have had, if they still exist, now that their reputation precedes them. One wrong decision with powerful, life-altering consequences.

YOUR TURN 1.1

Know Your Own Internet Presence

Directions: 1) Log on to the Internet and do a general search for your name. Do you find any information that you are not expecting? Are there other people with the same name as you who may be portraying an image that is questionable? If so, you may want to actually make a note of this on

---

[vii] Nathanson, H. "Harvard Rescinds Acceptances for at Least Ten Students for Obscene Memes." *The Harvard Crimson.* 5 June 2017. Web. http://www.thecrimson.com/article/2017/6/5/2021-offers-rescinded-memes/

college or job applications so as to avoid any misunderstandings about who you are.

2) Make a list of any social media accounts you use. Review the information you have out there on those various platforms. Be sure there aren't old posts that you'd want to remove as you have grown older and matured. Think about things like strong or political opinions you may have shared. While of course everyone is entitled to her own thoughts and beliefs, sometimes it is best not to make everything you think public.

In your elementary and middle school years if you had good communication skills they likely led to strong family relationships and friendships and positive relationships with coaches, teachers, and administrators. If your communication skills were lacking, you may have had some struggles, but it is never too late to make improvements! As you get older, good communication skills can lead to positive relationships with college roommates, professors, and advisors, and eventually strong communication and self-presentation skills can serve you well in the work world. When we don't have a lot of life experience to work with, we sometimes don't realize how important communicating and being well received can be. Focusing on good communication skills is an investment in your future.

Here are some tasks where strong communication and self-presentation skills can have an impact:

- Having strong and healthy relationships with friends and family
- Being recommended for higher level coursework, internships, workshops, or conferences
- Being selected for a leadership role within a sport, club, group, or activity in which you participate
- Obtaining quality letters of recommendation for college, graduate school, or employment
- Interviewing for part-time jobs, college, graduate school, or your first job
- Networking at college and/or career fairs
- Earning a promotion or advancement in the workplace

1.7: Communication, Self-Presentation, and Entering the Workforce

Because the nature of communication has changed so dramatically over the last few decades, differences in communication styles between different generations coexisting in the work world has become a hot topic. Since many high school students enter the workforce through a part-time job, and most students eventually have a full-time job, having an understanding of differences in communication styles is important! In the article, "Today's Generations Face New Communication Gaps," featured in the Jobs section of *USA Today*, author Denise Kersten defines the generations, their differing styles of communication, and what they value in the workplace.[viii]

"Traditionalists" were born between 1922 and 1943. Since talking in person was the primary way to communicate for much of their lives, these employees value talking in person. But they also believe their time is important and to be respected, so many don't like an unexpected drop-in. They prefer that you schedule time to meet with them.

"Baby boomers" were born between 1943 and 1960. Baby boomers also lived during a time where most communication happened in person or over the phone. They believe in building personable relationships and want to receive recognition for their success, so showing appreciation and respect for wisdom they may impart is important.

"Generation X" was born between 1960 and 1980. This generation grew up with some modern conveniences such as remote controls. Cell phones and the Internet came into existence during their college or early workdays. Therefore, they have become accustomed to quick and efficient forms of communication such as email.

"Generation Y" or "millennials" were born between 1980 and 2002. Many millennials were raised by dual working parents who sacrificed greatly to enhance their careers, requiring long work hours which often extended into evenings and weekends. Seeing the impact of this work style, this generation values work–life balance. Many things have been instantaneous for those of the millennial generation, and it can easily be forgotten that the prior generations are not used to communicating via IM and text. So though your peers may be used to texting and instant responses, you cannot assume that all others that you work with will be.

[viii] Kersten, D. "Today's Generations Face New Communication Gaps." *USA Today.* 15 November 2002. Web. http://usatoday30.usatoday.com/money/jobcenter/workplace/communication/2002-11-15-communication-gap_x.htm

Jean Twenge, author of iGen, has suggested that there is a new generation comprised of those born after 1995, called the "iGen." While they may overlap with the youngest millennials, they have some defining characteristics that will certainly add a new component to future workplaces. Since the Internet exploded in 1995, the iGen has grown up with the Internet, computers, tablets, and cell phones. They only know a world where they have been immersed in screens and technology. According to Twenge, the biggest difference between iGen and previous generations is how they prefer to spend their time, which is on a device, usually their phone, and on social media. This has led to less face-to-face interactions; thus, social skills and communication may be less developed. The iGen values individualism and can be accepting of everybody. They are very concerned about physical and emotional safety because their screen viewing has given them easy access to the frightening coverage of incidences of school and world violence, which can make some in this generation hesitant to take risks. iGen'ers will bring a perspective about communicating in school and the workforce that will be very different than their predecessors, and will require a joint effort by all generations to create an effective and collaborative learning or work environment.

A potential disconnect between generations in the workplace was described by author Shannon Gausepohl in her article "Tackling 4 Key Challenges of the Multigenerational Workforce," which ran in *Business News Daily*.[ix] Gausepohl shares that many baby boomers and Generation X'ers believe that millennials are lazy, entitled, and tech-obsessed because they were raised in a world where much of what they wanted to access was instantly available to them. On the other hand, she says that millennials think of the older generations as stubborn and set in their ways. Amy Casciotti, Vice President of Human Resources for TechSmith Corporation, says, "We should all seek out other perspectives and ways of thinking and that includes others from different age groups. Diverse thinking is critical to all organizations." Allen Shayanfekr, CEO and cofounder of Sharestates, agrees that communication is key. "Always respect your team, no matter their age. Speak to them. Make sure they're learning and happy in their work environment."

[ix] Gausepohl, S. "Tackling 4 Key Challenges of the Multigenerational Workforce." *Business News Daily*. 5 December 2016. Web. http://www.businessnewsdaily.com/6609-multigenerational-workforce-challenges.html

1.8: Even Hollywood Thinks This Is an Important Topic!

In the movie *The Intern*, Robert DeNiro stars as a retired, successful business owner and widower who lands an internship at a fashion website run by a young, career-driven wife and mother, Anne Hathaway. Though there were some rough patches and laughable moments, the movie provides an accurate commentary about how all generations can learn from each other to run a successful business. DeNiro brings his skills that were honed over a 50-year career in the business world in a time when men dressed in business suits and carried briefcases. He learns from his new, young colleagues how to set up email, Facebook, and adopt a more informal approach to the workday. They, on the other hand, learn many admirable traits and a work ethic from him. The movie makes the important point that even though there were some challenges and growing pains for all involved, when everyone has an open mind and is willing to learn something new, everyone can benefit.[x]

1.9: But Don't Get Too Caught Up in Hollywood!

Though *The Intern* imparts some valuable words of wisdom, there are also some conflicting messages being delivered to you as growing, maturing, young adults. A prominent genre otherwise known as "reality TV" has been on the rise for some time now. If you were to get caught up in watching these shows, you might see a different type of value system being reinforced. Oftentimes these shows are about winning, about being the "last man standing," and about knocking everyone and anyone else down along the way to get to the top. Other times, the shows are about being as outrageous or provocative as possible and earning a paycheck while doing so. While these shows often provide real viewing drama and great ratings for networks, the communication and self-presentation skills on display are typically not ones which would lead to a successful existence in most other settings in the world, so it might be best to leave the cheating, gossiping,

[x] Costas, C. & Mnuchin, S. (Producers), & Meyers, N. (Director). (2015). *The Intern* [Motion Picture]. United States: Warner Bros.

and backstabbing to the world of reality TV and not bring it into your own reality!

Having good communication skills and the ability to understand how one is perceived are very important to being successful in life. The good news is that it is never too late to focus on mastering these skills. Armed with strong communication and self-presentation skills, students can take control of their today, tomorrow, and future.

1.10: The Take Away

- Communication involves giving and receiving information.
- Communication comes in many forms and having mastery of those can lead to more successful relationships and life experiences.
- Have an awareness of how you are perceived by others.
- Take charge of your social media presence, and be sure your image is one that you are proud of.
- Remember that different generations value different forms of communication, so try to be flexible in your own communication styles when it can impact relationships (especially in your education and in the workforce).

HOW SOCIAL SKILLS GOT LEFT BEHIND

C an you think back to when you started school as a kindergartener? Do you have any memories of your teacher, your classroom, a special project, or making new friends? Maybe you were a little scared or a little worried. After all, you would be leaving home, even if only for a few hours. Perhaps you had to ride a big, yellow bus with a bunch of kids you didn't know, or maybe you had to try a snack that consisted of unknown food choices! There were many unknowns as you moved forward on a 12-year journey that would provide challenges, frustrations, learning experiences, and much joy along the way. Little did you know that many of the most important lessons you'd learn in life were actually learned in kindergarten.

So important were those lessons that author Robert Fulghum actually wrote a book called, *All I Ever Needed to Know I Learned in Kindergarten*. "Share everything. Play fair. Don't hit people. Put things back where you found them. Clean up your own mess. Don't take things that aren't yours. Say you're sorry when you hurt somebody. Wash your hands before you eat. Flush. Live a balanced life. Learn some and think some. Draw and paint and sing and dance. Play and work every day some. Take a nap every afternoon. When you go out into the world, watch out for traffic. Hold hands and stick together. Be aware of wonder."[i]

Those days when you were in kindergarten, education focused on the three Rs: reading, writing, and 'rithmetic, but there were also many opportunities to learn and practice life lessons.

In the early school days, social skills and work habits were so important that, in fact, they used to be formally evaluated in great detail on report cards. At some private and parochial schools, they still remain a part of a student's performance evaluation even in high school! In many school settings, even in the younger years, there has been less of an emphasis on social skills due to an increased pressure to focus on academic skills via standardized testing. Author Thomas Sterner, in his book *The Practicing Mind,* shares that he feels something important has been lost as society has chosen to focus on the product over the process. By focusing only on outcomes, such as strong test results, what gets lost is any reward for focusing on the joy of learning as something valuable in and of itself.[ii] There is a growing body of literature that makes the case that focusing on "soft skills" such as good communication or good citizenship should be just as important as an "A" on a calculus exam.

2.1: So What Are Those Soft Skills?

These skills might include cooperation, respect, manners, responsibility, self-control, empathy, kindness, listening attentively, attending to and completing tasks, following directions, persevering, good problem-solving skills, creativity, accepting constructive suggestions, bouncing back after a failure or disappointment, self-confidence, humbleness, integrity, and class participation. Many parents, teachers, and employers still feel these are the skills that are the most important for raising a well-rounded, successful individual—a person any organization would want to recruit, accept, or hire! You may also recognize that these skills are important!

[i] Fulghum, R. *Everything I Ever Really Needed to Know I Learned in Kindergarten.* Evanston, IL: Press of Ward Schori, 1988.
[ii] Sterner, T. M. *The Practicing Mind: Developing Focus and Discipline in Your Life. Novato,* CA: New World Library, 2012.

2.2: What Happened to Them?

In your early elementary years, there was likely some focus on behavior and social skills; however, as you entered middle and high school you may never have heard about those skills again because they probably weren't evaluated on your report card or built into some grade. In middle school, there was a shift from a focus on the process to the product (data, numbers, grades, rank). Those lessons that might have been learned in kindergarten, those lifelong skills that need to continue to grow and be nurtured in order to be a successful student and employee, have been overtaken by ramped-up academic expectations and coursework. While they still may be valued, there is less time to focus on them during the school day. But practice makes perfect, and so while you may not be required to focus on social skills any longer, you can still choose to focus on them voluntarily!

VOICES FROM CAMPUS 2.1

Try Not To Succumb To The Pressure...

Sarah: I just finished working on my course selection sheet for my junior year classes. Did you do yours yet?

Janie: Yes, my mom just signed off on it.

Sarah: What are you taking?

Janie: Two APs, two honors, and the rest are college prep level or electives.

Sarah: Oh, I just signed up for three APs and three honors. My mom said that she's been talking to the neighbors and I have no chance of getting into a competitive college unless I take three APs as a junior and probably four or more as a senior. I am feeling so stressed about it. I feel like I am going to have to drop out of sports and clubs to have enough time to do homework.

Janie: I met with my guidance counselor and he said that colleges and universities want to see a well-rounded student, not just one with straight As in all APs. He said that I have to make more time for volunteer work and other clubs, and also that it is important to have work–life balance.

Sarah: That sounds a lot better than what I am signing on for. Maybe I can have another talk with my mom.

Yes, even parents can easily get caught up in the whirlwind of high school course selections and college preparation and applications as they worry about the future of their children. In talking to many students and parents, there seems to be an unspoken expectation that stresses the importance of taking an abundance of honors and AP courses because "they say we should." When pushed to tell who "they" are, many students don't have a concrete answer. It's not always their parents, school counselor, or teachers. It seems that there is an underlying competitive expectation that students (or parents) perceive, and they get so caught up in the whirlwind of higher grades, class rank, and prepping for their academic future that they lose sight of those important skills that were learned in kindergarten and, perhaps, what really matters for future success and happiness. If you can find a career that allows you to use your strengths doing something you love, you will never work a day in your life. Good social and communication skills apply in all arenas, so consider the advice of a TV personality, Mike Rowe, who is known for his work on The Discovery Channel and CNN. He says that currently 54 percent of the available jobs are in the skilled trades and that the jobs that exist right now do not require massive college debt.[iii] Remember there is no one future set in stone; trust your gut instincts. If college doesn't feel right for you, investigate all options for post–high school learning opportunities—that can include learning a trade or other résumé-building experiences such as traveling abroad, participating in mission work, apprenticeships, etc.

The curriculum and academic expectations have changed in our schools, and as a result there is less time to focus on those critical social skills. Additionally, the abundant use of technology has resulted in less in-person communication, and this has reduced the opportunity to practice social skills.

Before the explosion of technology, people *had* to communicate face to face … not FaceTime to FaceTime or behind a screen. There was more personal interaction, which allowed for seeing a person's reaction to a comment, whether it was joyful, surprised, or upset. People talked more. There was more give and take in a conversation, which allowed for more reflective and thoughtful communication. With less time spent behind a screen, there were more social interactions, which helped develop better social skills. Greeting people by name, making eye contact, asking the questions how are you or how can I help, and getting to know others on a deeper level

iii Rowe, M. "The Jobs that Exist Right Now Don't Require Massive College Debt." *ATTN:*. 27 May 2017. Web. https://www.facebook.com/attn/videos/1388355794533209/

were commonplace. People spent more time in nature, reading, participating in physical activities, playing games, and overall, more time with family and friends. Families shared a meal together and talked about their day. When friends and family went out to dinner, they talked to each other. When going for a car ride, people talked to each other, played a game, or listened to music. In the business world, when waiting for a meeting to start, employees chatted and got to know each a little better. All of these examples are how communication and social skills developed ... naturally. It just happened.

And then came the screens. As more people communicated more through screens, communication changed. Yes, sometimes this instant communication is quite helpful. But other times it can lead to miscommunication and hurt feelings. There are some occasions where direct face-to-face conversation is best. With the onset of technology, the level of empathy is reported to have decreased. Empathy is a critical lifelong skill—one of those important life lessons. With empathy, the world is a better place. Without it, there could be an increase in bullying and hurt feelings and less happiness.

YOUR TURN 2.1

Are Devices A Big Part Of Your Life?

Directions: Keep track of your use of any electronic device for one or two days. Record the device, amount of time, and the reason for using it. Evaluate the effectiveness of its use. Do you notice any trends? Did you miss out on doing something else because you were on a device (being with a friend or family member, eating a meal, sleeping, doing homework, being outside, being active in a sport or recreational activity, etc.)?

Date	Purpose	Device	Total Time	End Time	Start Time	Effective/ Got the Job Done

Pick one device that you use regularly and agree to turn it off for 24 hours. Record what you did instead. How hard was it to disconnect? Did you try something new or something you haven't done for a while?

Total Time in Activity	End Time	Start Time	Alternate Activity	Disconnected Device

Reflection
- How hard was it for you to disconnect from this device?
- Did you find that you became anxious when it wasn't available?
- Was there any positive outcome from this experience? Did you try something new or something you haven't done for a while?
- Would you have been able to remain disconnected longer than 24 hours?

In addition, text messages do not allow for developing deeper level communication skills. Text messages tend to be abbreviated and brief with little regard to punctuation or spelling. Although email allows for lengthier communication and more proper grammar and spelling, one has to check email, and many younger people don't. For some situations, texting and email are an efficient way of communicating, but relying on only texting for most of your communication could have long-term effects.

VOICES FROM CAMPUS 2.2

Learn From Eric…

Consider the story of a senior who had stellar grades and had applied to many colleges. He completed the applications, wrote his essays, and his parents paid the application fees. And then he waited. Basketball season started, midterms began, and spring break was right around the corner. One day, his counselor saw him in the hall …

Counselor: Eric, nice game! By the way, have you heard from any of your schools yet?

Eric: Nah, I guess it's too early.

Counselor: Not really. You should have heard by now, even if it is to say your application is complete or provide more information about financial aid.

Eric: I know. My mom keeps bugging me about finding out more about financial aid.

Counselor: Have you checked your email?

Eric: No. I never check it.

Eric learned an important lesson that day. When he went home and checked his email, there were many unopened emails from many schools. Included in one of those emails was an acceptance to one of his favorite schools along with a financial aid and scholarship application … that was due in a few days! Good thing he saw his counselor in the hall. Unfortunately he also discovered that he had missed two very important emails. One was inviting him to do an interview, but he had missed the deadline to schedule one, and in another he had missed the deadline to apply for a very large scholarship.

College professors are reporting that they rarely hear from students and often sit alone during office hours. Their students will email them with a question but don't usually come in and meet with them in person. In fact, some students expect to text their professors, which may or may not be welcomed. While many students have a strong comfort level with texting, remember from Chapter 1 that many of the older generations do not. So while students might feel like they are doing a great deal to communicate with their professors, their professors may perceive just the opposite—they may view the students' behavior as avoidance. Yikes! That could have an impact on a final grade!

Most people who become teachers do so because they enjoy working with kids and young adults. They like being in a helping profession. They want to spend time talking with and getting to know you. Let them! The more time you spend with your teachers, the more they will know you. The more they know you, the more you will stand out in their minds. This can be a big help if you ever need their help with their course because they will recognize that you are trying and you care (perhaps you'll even get some brownie points for effort). It will also give you practice talking to adults, perhaps even when it's uncomfortable. You will have to do this often in future situations. Don't forget that there are many other opportunities for networking with caring adults. For example, you might get involved at your church, community center, community service outreach program, Scouts, or other activity outside of school. Perhaps a coach or supervisor at a part-time job will prove to be a great mentor and friend. The more you practice interacting with a variety of people, the easier it will become.

It can also help to get to know adults who are in the field that you might want to pursue. Talk to them about why they chose that career. Spend time shadowing them. They can be of great help, if you just get to know them. You can't develop these kinds of relationships behind a screen. Electronic communication can be a starting point and a means of exchanging information, but it can never take the place of in-person, face-to-face communication.

2.3: Social Skills and Work Habits Matter

So let's go back and look at why those skills can offer such value to you now as a high school and college student. To quote Ted Dintersmith, author of *America Desperately Needs to Redefine 'College and Career Ready,'* "Our education goals have lost touch with what matters most—helping students develop essential skills, competencies, and character traits. It's time to reimagine the goals for U.S. education, and hold all schools—from kindergarten through college—accountable for teaching the skills and nurturing the dispositions most needed for learning, work, and citizenship."[iv]

2.4: What Are These Important Skills?

Google's chairman and head of hiring, Laszlo Bock, says that he doesn't care what degrees a student has. At one point he even said, "GPAs are worthless as a criteria for hiring, and test scores are worthless.... We found that they don't predict anything. Humans are by nature creative beings, but not by nature logical, structured-thinking beings. Those are skills you have to learn." A degree doesn't really tell what an individual can do. A degree will give you expertise in a subject, but what you want are skills and experience. Some employers would even say that there is too much emphasis on book learning versus real-world learning. They are looking for workers who possess a blend of technology skills and "soft skills." Google chairman, Eric Schmidt, says, "It looks like the thing that separates out the capable students from the really

[iv] Dintersmith, T. & Wagner, T. "America Desperately Needs to Redefine 'College and Career Ready.'" *MarketWatch.* 31 August 2016. Web. http://www.marketwatch.com/story/america-desperately-needs-to-re-define-college-and-career-ready-2016-08-05

successful ones is not so much their knowledge … but their persistence at something." Bock is more interested in looking at skills than a degree, and he ranks these skills from most important to least important:[v]

1. Ability to learn (we would add willingness to learn)
2. Leadership
3. Humility
4. Ownership and responsibility for solving problems
5. Expertise in the subject matter

CareerBuilder, in a 2015 article, reported that the skills recent graduates lack and what employers are actually looking for include (in order from greatest to least):

1. Interpersonal or people skills (commonly known as social skills)
2. Strong problem solving
3. Oral communication
4. Leadership
5. Written communication
6. Teamwork
7. Creative thinking
8. Project management
9. Research and analysis ability
10. Math skills
11. Computer and technology skills

Do you notice some similarities between these lists and what you learned in kindergarten? Many other college admissions staff and company CEO's recognize that successful people seem to possess these and other similar character traits, traits that they are now looking for in future students and employees. Traits that could be considered the valued soft skills that need to accompany the knowledge and expertise in an area of study. So what are the other skills that matter?

[v] Ferenstein, G. "Why Google Doesn't Care About College Degrees, in 5 Quotes." *VentureBeat.* 25 April 2014. Web. 5 April 2017. https://venturebeat.com/2014/04/25/why-google-doesnt-care-about-college-degrees-in-5-quotes/

1. Self-confident but humble—a big and small ego both in the same person

2. Creative thinker and problem solver

3. Perseverance/grit/resilience—can you bounce back after a failure or disappointment?

4. Self-motivated and self-starter but will ask for help when needed

5. Good listener

6. Accepts constructive feedback

7. Respect/good manners

We left this one for last because depending on where, when, and how you were raised, your perception of what constitutes good manners and respect may be different. No matter the time or the place, the "magic words" that you were taught in kindergarten still matter. Please, thank you, you're welcome, and excuse me are still noticed and appreciated. In fact, believe it or not, college admission folks and HR personnel say they STILL appreciate receiving a handwritten thank you note. It shows that you care enough to take the time to thank someone for taking the time to help you—and that can help you stand out!

Eye contact is another important social skill that shows respect in most cultures. But be aware, in some cultures, eye contact can be seen as a sign of disrespect, especially when a younger person is being spoken to by an elder. However, for most of the intent of this guide, making eye contact with the person to whom you are speaking will be valued.

Using a person's name demonstrates that you took the time to listen and remember. It will make him feel valued, and you will be remembered.

In some businesses, sharing a meal can be a way of assessing a candidate's poise, grace, and manners. Many decisions and deals are made while "breaking bread," and a lot can be learned about an individual by observing his manners at the table. So ... remember what you learned in kindergarten. Napkin in your lap and use your utensils. And while you didn't learn this next tip in kindergarten, it is just as important. Put your cell phone away, and enjoy a face-to-face conversation with your potential boss or client.

YOUR TURN 2.2

Rate Yourself

Directions: Below you will find a report card that evaluates behaviors that are critical in today's workplace and what employers are searching for in their new employees. Rate yourself and then ask others to rate you. Perhaps consider asking a peer and an older adult (parent, relative, neighbor, teacher, coach, or boss). The more perspectives, the better! See if the ratings are similar. If not, where do they differ and why? Are there behaviors that you might want to develop? Can you do it on your own or might you want to ask others for suggestions, especially if they are areas that you were unaware of?

Grading Key:
All of the Personal and Social Growth and Work Habits/Effort descriptors are graded on a scale of 1, 2, or 3. 1 = needs improvement, 2 = satisfactory, 3 = outstanding

Personal and Social Growth			
Respectful			
Uses manners			
Cooperative			
Responsible			
Self-controlled			
Empathetic			
Generosity/service for others			
Work Habits/Effort			
Attends to and completes tasks on time			
Demonstrates perseverance			
Listens attentively			
Follows directions			
Participates in discussions			
Seeks out resources to solve problems			
Can work independently or with a team			
Accepts constructive feedback			

Is able to bounce back from a setback and try again			
Asks for help			
Manages time efficiently			
Manages materials efficiently			

2.5: The Take Away

- Take advantage of opportunities to build relationships with and seek guidance from a variety of people, including your teachers, coaches, spiritual leaders, community volunteers, employers, and of course, family and friends.

- Use those relationships and opportunities to develop those "soft skills" and characteristics and broaden your perspectives in a supportive environment.

- Take time to greet people, make eye contact, use their name, and demonstrate that you really do care.

- Find a balance when using technology so that it doesn't interfere with developing and using social skills.

- While expertise and knowledge about a given subject matter are important, school and college personnel and those who hire in the business world are looking for the same skills that you learned in kindergarten.

CHAPTER

3

SHIFT IN AUTONOMY: WHO'S IN CHARGE?

hild development theory, something you would learn if you took Psychology 101, tells us that as children grow into young adults there should be a shift in autonomy. Well, what does autonomy mean? Autonomy is defined as freedom from external control or influence; independence. When children are young, they lack the physical capability, the decision-making skills, responsibility, and maturity to take care of themselves. Young children are dependent on their parents for all their needs to be met. Parents provide physical care and emotional support. They take care of daily needs such as transportation to and from preschool and school or activities, and they have conferences with teachers, as needed. However as you grow older, some of the responsibility for daily routines can and should be shifted to you. For example, during preschool and early elementary school, you should be able to clean up your own mess. By mid elementary school, you should be able to help with basic chores around the house, and by late elementary you could potentially pack your own lunch or prepare a basic snack. In middle school, you might take on more household chores, and by late middle school you could have many responsibilities, such as mowing the yard, watching your younger siblings until your mom or dad get home from work, and maybe even cooking dinner for the family.

In schools across America, toward the end of elementary school and during middle school, students are encouraged to understand their strengths and weaknesses and to be able to speak to their teacher about their needs. After all, in middle school and high school you lose the comfort of having that one elementary teacher who "knows" you, and instead you have potentially five or more different teachers to get to know, and they have to get to know you! High school students are expected to be able to do many things to care for themselves physically and emotionally, and it is expected that you be able to advocate for yourself via conversations with guidance counselors and teachers.

3.1: A Change in Autonomy Trends

Students are supposed to gain autonomy as they grow older; however, some trends being identified by educators and researchers are showing that this process is not happening as it is supposed to, and as it once did quite successfully for decades. In her book *How to Raise an Adult,* Julie Lythcott-Haims, former Dean of Freshman at Stanford University, reports that high school teachers, college administrators, and employers are saying that many of the young people they are teaching or working with are unable to recognize their own strengths and weaknesses and are unable to advocate for themselves, showing that level of autonomy that is expected.[i] Your generation has been raised by loving and caring but sometimes over-involved parents, and now some young people may not know how to be independent—or at least find that it can be very challenging or cause a rise in anxiety as they try to take on more responsibility. So why the shift? Many attribute it to changes in our culture. Because the news is so accessible via multi-TV households and the Internet, parents are made more aware of things like kidnappings or the amount of child predators living in their community, making parents feel more fearful about their child's safety. Technology has made it easy for people to access one another. In the "old times" parents had to make a phone call, wait to receive one in return, or even schedule a conference. Email has allowed parents to easily contact their child's coach over playing time or a teacher over a missed assignment or grade or to express displeasure over something. While many parents are becoming over-involved out of fear, you, as an emerging young adult,

[i] Lythcott-Haims, J. *How to Raise an Adult: Break Free of the Overparenting Trap and Prepare Your Kid for Success.* New York: Saint Martin's Griffin, 2016.

may believe that it means your parents don't think you are good enough or competent enough or smart enough to do it by yourself.

VOICES FROM CAMPUS 3.1

It's Time to Make The Shift...

Consider these two scenarios:

As a child, Gina wasn't allowed to ride her bike down the street to a friend's house, take gymnastics for fear she'd get hurt, and wasn't allowed to sleep over at a friend's house until middle school. Whenever there was a problem with her friends, Gina's mom would try to help by calling the teacher or the other child's mother. Gina's mom was also very involved in checking her homework and select-ed all her high school classes for her. She went online constantly to check assignments and grades even knowing them before Gina got off the bus in the afternoon. When Gina entered college, she did fine academically but struggled to make decisions, speak up in class, and form relationships with faculty members and classmates. She often called her mom to get advice on life's daily problems, or her mom would call her to check up on how her day was going or to find out where she was. Shortly into her first semester, Gina realized that there was a big problem. "It got to the point where I didn't know how to talk to people," said Gina. "I was depressed. I had to learn how to stand on my own two feet and not always rely on my mom."

Or this less dramatic, yet regular occurrence in high school classrooms across America:

High school student: "I remember being mortified when my math teacher pulled me aside to ask why my mom had emailed him to say that I was really struggling with the homework assignment and would need more time to prepare for the upcoming test. He said if I had approached him, he would have been happy to help me." In hindsight, this student realized that it really was kind of silly that his mom had emailed the teacher. He really should have tried to talk with the teacher first. After all, asking for help is no big deal!

"Who IS the boss of you?" This is a common question that is asked in elementary school, and the correct answer would be "I am." However, the reality is that for the longest time your parents were, so the shift to taking responsibility for yourself is not necessarily a clear or easy one. According to author Dr. Wendy Mogul, in her bestseller *The Blessing of a Skinned Knee*, over the last 10–15 years, parents seem to be staying in charge of their children longer than is necessary or good.[ii] Teachers, professors, and even employers have reported increased communication with parents rather than the young adults whom they teach or might employ.

VOICES FROM CAMPUS 3.2

Parents Mean Well But…

Consider how in the following scenarios, Mom or Dad may have overstepped their boundaries.

"Can you believe that her mother called to ask if she could have an extension on the project's due date?" said the high school history teacher.

Father to a high school math teacher: "Can't you just give him the benefit of the doubt and change his grade to an A rather than a B+? It will help his GPA."

Admissions officer to a friend: "I got another phone call from a parent whose son wasn't accepted. She demanded to know why he wasn't considered and could we reconsider."

After being hired by a healthcare organization, a young woman sat through an in-depth discussion of healthcare and other benefits. At the end of the day, rather than turning in her forms, the young woman asked if she could take the paperwork home. The next morning, the human resource manager got a phone call from the young woman's mother.

Mother of newly hired employee: "My daughter doesn't understand it and is afraid of you. There's no way she can come back and ask you these questions, so I need to ask them and then I can help her."[iii]

Teach for America, an organization that provides a source of teachers in largely urban, underfunded school districts where

ii Mogel, W. *The Blessing of a Skinned Knee: Using Jewish Teachings to Raise Self-reliant Children.* New York: Scribner, 2008.

poverty and its impact are very obvious, typically hires people who demonstrate grit and resilience because they will need those skills to get the job done. However, this is a conversation that is more typical than ever before:

Parent: "This is an inappropriate placement for my daughter. She is working with a totally incompetent principal, and you need to switch her employment. This would never happen in my company/school."[iv]

3.2: It's Hard for Mom and Dad to Let Go ...

At some point, what teenagers or young adults don't value being free and independent of their parents? Most teens want to have a later curfew, learn to drive a car, or want to decide what college to attend or job to take. So if teens and young adults want their autonomy so badly, then why are parents not letting go? Many books have been written on the subject. Here are some of the explanations offered: some parents want to relive their lives vicariously through their son or daughter, others don't want to see their child be unhappy or frustrated, still others might view their child as a project (one that requires constant work), and many parents just have trouble letting go. It can be very hard, even painful, for some parents. They may be scared—scared that they aren't needed anymore or scared for their children's safety and future. However, the greatest gifts parents can give their children are roots and wings. Wings to fly and wings to soar. Yes, on this flight you will make mistakes, maybe even crash and burn from time to time. But you will or already have learned from your mistakes. With experience come wisdom and the confidence to know that you are capable and independent. You can rise above and solve your problems. You will tuck away all of these life experiences and rely on them for future challenges and whatever life hands you.

[iii] Lythcott-Haims, J. *How to Raise an Adult: Break Free of the Overparenting Trap and Prepare Your Kid for Success.* New York: Saint Martin's Griffin, 2016.
[iv] Lythcott-Haims, J. *How to Raise an Adult: Break Free of the Overparenting Trap and Prepare Your Kid for Success.* New York: Saint Martin's Griffin, 2016.

3.3: A Humorous Reflection on Gaining Autonomy

If you are never given the chance to develop autonomy, you will stay reliant on others, which is no way to become an adult. In the movie *Failure to Launch*, Matthew McConaughey plays a man well into adulthood who does not want to "leave the nest." His mother, played by Joanne Bates, is initially flattered by her son's desire to remain at home. She has doted on him her whole life. However, at some point she grows tired of the extra work involved with him remaining at home. She hires a "launch consultant," played by Sarah Jessica Parker, to lure him out of the home and teach him that he should actually want to gain independence. What ensues is a bunch of laughable moments! [v] At the end of the day, we can all find a little humor in our situation. Whether you have chosen to remain dependent on your parents or you parents have encouraged it, perhaps now is the time to reflect on whether that is really a good lifelong choice!

3.4: Independence and Good Social Skills Are Critical to Success

A theory called the "self-determination theory" holds that every person has three basic needs in order to be happy: she must feel autonomous, competent, and connected to other people. Autonomy, independence, and problem solving go hand in hand and result in feelings of competence. With good social skills comes a feeling of being connected to other people. When these critical skills are not developed, happiness is hard to achieve. [vi]

It is also critical that people develop a skill called self-efficacy. It is the extent or strength of one's belief in one's own ability to complete tasks and reach goals. If you can set goals and then do whatever it takes to achieve your goals, then you are demonstrating self-efficacy. You have to believe in yourself.

[v] Bozman, R. (Producer), & Dey,T. (Director). (2006). *Failure to Launch* [Motion Picture]. United States: Paramount.

[vi] Rochman, B. "Hover No More: Helicopter Parents May Breed Depression and Incompetence in Their Children." *Time.* 22 February 2013. Web. 26 February 2017. http://healthland.time.com/2013/02/22/ hover-no-more-helicopter-parents-may-breed-depression-and-incompetence-in-their-children/

What Happens When Those Skills Are Not Mastered?

Even though many young adults are fortunate enough to go to college, many employers are recognizing a disconnect between college and career readiness and have concerns about some critical skills that are lacking in their younger employees, such as oral and written expression, collaboration, problem solving, and perseverance. They report that young people seem to lack something, and that lack gets in the way of being able to self-reflect, present their best selves, and communicate in thoughtful and meaningful ways. They often don't see all that they are and have to offer, and therefore they may not communicate that to prospective schools or organizations. Thus, it's critical that parents and teachers encourage you to practice responsibility and independence from a young age. This way, as you enter middle and high school, you will be more comfortable advocating for your needs, speaking to teachers, and expressing yourself accurately and respectfully. If you have developed these critical life skills over time, they will be in your comfort zone when you are in high school and beyond and expected to use them.

3.5: So How Can I Be More Independent?

There are many skills that go into being an independent, autonomous young person, and they can begin to develop as early as the toddler years. The best practice for learning any new skill involves people modeling the skill for you, then you practice it with their help and eventually you can do it independently. The more you demonstrate these skills independently, the easier it will be for your parents to back off.

As you read over these questions, see how many times you answer yes. The more yes responses, the easier it should be for your parent(s) to recognize that you are on your way to being an autonomous being. If you need constant reminders, you are making it harder for your parents to back off, even though they should do it anyway and let you learn from logical consequences.

When you are willing and enthusiastic students or employees, no one will need to hover over you or act on your behalf. You will be an asset to any class or company.

Responsibility

Do you take responsibility for yourself, your homework, and your personal items?

Do you do assigned chores without reminders? Do you see what needs to be done and do it without being asked?

The more you can do for yourself and contribute to the family, the more you will prove to your parents that you are, indeed, very capable.

Respect

Are you able to engage in respectful conversations with people of all ages? If you have a concern, are you able to discuss it with a parent without getting in his or her face or stomping out the door when you don't get your way?

The calmer you stay and the more willing you are to listen and give and take, the more likely your parent will recognize that you are growing up!

Conflict Resolution

Are you able to resolve minor conflicts with friends without parental involvement?

The more you can deal with friend issues without parental involvement, the more you will be able to handle future relationship issues with college roommates or co-workers.

Communication Skills

How comfortable are you asking a teacher for help (moving a seat, help with an assignment) or if you question a grade on a test?

Can you seek out the help of a guidance counselor about course selection or a personal problem?

Can you access information about a question or problem via Internet or phone? Even though in today's world most information can be found and needs can be satisfied online, it's important that you are capable of and comfortable with having a phone conversation with a stranger.

Persistence and Determination

Do you have that quality of "stick-to-it-ness" or do you give up easily when the going gets tough?

When things become tough or you fail, do you pick yourself back up and start over again until you figure it out or solve the problem?

Do you set goals and develop a plan to achieve those goals?

If you are setting goals and following through to achieve them, then it's obvious that you don't need someone to do it for you. Might you need the occasional piece of advice from a trusted adult? Of course. But it's still your road, your path, and your life.

Or are you following your parents' goals for you? Do you say "I'm applying to Podunk University," or do you hear your parents say, "We are applying to Podunk University"?

Whose goals are they? They should be yours, and perhaps you could respectfully remind your loving parents of that.[vii]

Participation With Enthusiasm

Do you willingly participate in class, extracurricular activities, family events, and life in general, and do you do so with enthusiasm? Is there a sense of wanting to learn or do versus having to learn or do?

Attention/Focus/Effort

These three tend to go hand in hand. If you can put forth effort on your own, then you will not need Mom or Dad to push you.

YOUR TURN 3.1

How Independent Are You?

Directions: Autonomy develops increased attention and focus, effort, persistence, diligence, and participation, and hopefully leads to an enthusiastic student or employee. How autonomous are you now? Are there any areas that you may want to improve? Evaluate your autonomy in 10 categories. You might want to review your answers with one or two adults. Sometimes we are not aware of how others perceive us, so it's always a good idea to see if our own evaluations are in sync with those of others.[viii]

[vii] Lythcott-Haims, J. *How to Raise an Adult: Break Free of the Overparenting Trap and Prepare Your Kid for Success.* New York: Saint Martin's Griffin, 2016.

[viii] Youth in Transition Project, Adolescent Autonomy Checklist. Web. http://www.sped.sbcsc.k12.in.us/PDF%20Files/tassessments/Independent%20Living/Adolescent%20Autonomy%20Checklist.pdf

Personal Care	Can Do Already	Needs Practice	Need to Start
Choose appropriate clothes			
Manage personal hygiene			
Family/House			
Make bed including changing linens			
Dust, vacuum, and mop			
Clean bathroom			
Take out trash			
Weeding, raking leaves, lawn care			
Run errands for parent or self			
Kitchen			
Operate kitchen appliances and tools			
Go grocery shopping			
Plan and prepare meals			
Follow a recipe			
Set the table			
Do the dishes—by hand and operate dishwasher			
Laundry			
Sort clothes			
Operate washer and dryer			
Fold and put away clothes			
Iron clothes			
Healthcare			
Respond to medical questionnaire at appointments, therapy sessions, etc.			
Get a prescription filled			
Read a thermometer			
Know your medical coverage information			
Community			
Use public transportation			
Get a library or gym membership			

Use the post office			
How to locate a bathroom or other unfamiliar place			
How to handle a dispute (electric company, cable, phone, etc.)			
911 Emergency			
Use a fire extinguisher			
Know how to turn off water			
Know how to contact local police, EMS, and fire company			
Finances			
Develop a budget			
Open and manage a bank account (debit card, charge card, make deposits and withdrawals)			
Understand car and medical insurance and any student loans			
Understand how a lease works			
Can compute sales tax, tips, or discounts			
Now or Near Future			
Meet with school counselor/teacher/ mentor			
Check future options—military, trade school, apprenticeship, work,college (2-year or more)			
Complete a job application			
Ask a trusted adult to conduct a mock interview for a job or college application			
Apply for a job			
Write a thank you note to the person who interviewed you			

3.6: The Take Away

- School personnel and people in the workforce value students and employees who are independent and autonomous.
- Demonstrate respect and responsibility.
- Help your parents see that you are resilient, determined, and able to solve your problems and advocate for your needs.
- Being able to sustain focus and effort, follow through on responsibilities, and self-initiate to achieve your goals will demonstrate that you are well on your way to being an adult.

UNDERSTANDING THE ALMIGHTY RECOMMENDATION PROCESS!

Gosh, this is much more complicated than I realized!

While this chapter may seem geared toward high school students trying to obtain a recommendation — the advice is all still relevant to students in college who would need to potentially ask a professor for a recommendation in order to land an on or off campus job, internship, first job post graduation, or for graduate school.

I t seemed simple enough, get a letter of recommendation! But the student quoted above came to the above conclusion as a result of a brief encounter with his guidance counselor.

Counselor: So do you have any teachers in mind to write your recommendations?

Student: How many do I need?

Counselor: Well some colleges don't require a letter, others require one, and some strongly prefer two. Most schools that require recommendations prefer that they come from junior year teachers.

Student: Oh, hmmmm, I am not sure who to ask. I would love to ask my ninth grade biology teacher. I really loved that class.

Counselor: Unfortunately that letter may not help you all that much. I am sure you've changed a good deal from who you were as a ninth grade student. The admissions officers like to hear from junior year teachers because that information is fresh off the press—they hope that the letter will describe the student that you are today. So given this insight, is there any teacher from this year you might ask?

Student: Well, maybe my math teacher, or maybe my Computer Aided Drafting teacher ...

Counselor: The admissions counselors strongly prefer to hear from teachers in what we consider to be your "core courses": English, math, science, social studies, or foreign language. But if you have excelled in a specialty area or elective course such as art, computer programming, or engineering, sometimes a letter from a teacher in this area will work. It is important to research whether the colleges you are applying to have any specifications about teacher letters. For example, at some universities, if you are applying as an engineering major they require a letter from a math or science teacher, sometimes both.

All across America, in the spring of junior year, many school counselors and college counselors are meeting with juniors to perform what is known as a "Junior Planning Conference." Perhaps you have participated in a meeting where you learned about what is to come during the college application season, which takes place during the fall and winter of your senior year of high school. Some high schools do not have the staff to offer such a conference, and even at those that do, many students find themselves ill equipped to deal with the process of obtaining a letter of recommendation.

Many counselors have figured out that the spring of junior year is almost a bit late to be having a discussion about recommendations. The above dialogue is only the beginning of a discussion on the topic of recommendations. Students are then typically asked how they think their teachers will evaluate them. This question often yields more baffled replies. Counselors are finding that many students are feeling surprised and unprepared about how they will be evaluated.

At many high schools, the school counselor meets with his student roster once each year. Each year there is a different goal or purpose to the meeting. The purpose of the freshman meeting is often to see how the student is adjusting. Were the courses the student was taking a good fit?

Has the student thought about course selections for the following year? Has the student figured out how to join in on extracurricular activities? Does the student have any questions in general about what is to come during the remainder of high school? Students who receive such counseling sessions are lucky. In many schools across America where budgets are strained, a student may only see the guidance counselor if there is a problem.

For those students who wish to go on to college, beginning a discussion about college recommendations and the admissions process in general in the 11th grade can feel a little late. Planting the seeds of what is to come earlier in the high school experience can be a very effective technique. The process of reviewing an actual college recommendation form can be an eye opening and enlightening activity for many students. Armed with the knowledge that what a teacher thinks about them matters, students can take informed control of their relationships with teachers. Of course the goal of this activity is not to encourage students to form disingenuous relationships but rather to help students see that they are being watched and evaluated by their teachers and school administrators in many ways. Having this knowledge allows a student, often for the first time, to reflect on how he is being perceived. For many students, a discussion about the recommendation process will be the first time they learn that their actions have direct consequences in the form of a good, bad, or mediocre recommendation. Many students don't realize that their teachers do more than just give out grades!

4.1: Moving Through the Process

Since recommendations are a part of the college admissions process, all students are entitled to know what this process is all about. There should be no mystery. So let's consider the questions asked on a "typical" college recommendation form!

First, the form asks you to fill in basic information, such as your name, address, and the school you attend. Nowadays, this is typically done online. Therefore, you are typing in your answers.

Tip #1—Please check your typing for errors and be sure to use complete terminology. Because many students have grown up texting or using informal communication on apps like Snapchat, typos and abbreviations can happen, and they make a poor impression. For example, if the town you live in is named West Chester, putting W.C. for the city in the address slot would be frowned upon and reflect poorly on the student applicant.

Next, the form will typically ask if the student wants to "waive" his right to access the letter. It will mention something called FERPA (Family Education Right to Privacy Act). This is all about whether you will choose to have the right to see/view your letter at some point. You must answer this question with either a "yes" or "no."

Tip #2—While you, and you alone, must decide the correct answer for yourself, here is some insight into the question. First, at a great many high schools across America, it is the rule or unspoken expectation that students do not see or view the letters of recommendation. This is not because teachers write bad things about students, but more because the intention has always been that the letter goes straight from the teacher to the college admissions office and not through the student's hands. Typically if a teacher feels unable to write a positive letter, he will advise you to ask someone else. Students should think carefully about whom they choose to write their letter. If you feel comfortable asking the teacher, then there is likely to be little concern about negative content, and it should feel natural to waive your right to see it. This means that you trust the person who you have asked to write the letter, and this will give the college admissions officers greater confidence in the letter.

As an aside, many teachers give students a copy of their letter. Sometimes teachers do this as a way to let the students know how highly they thought of them. This is certainly a compliment when it happens. However, students should not be alarmed if the teacher does not provide them with a copy, as this does not mean there is something bad in the letter. School counselors will tell you that letters are typically complimentary. At worst, they could be perceived as kind but relatively neutral. Neutral letters can happen when a student hasn't really gone out of his way to get to know teachers or to excel or shine in any way in a classroom.

Talk to your school counselor to see if he has an opinion as to whom you might ask for a recommendation. Your counselor might be able to point you in the right direction!

VOICES FROM CAMPUS 4.1

Hard Work Can Pay Off...

It was one of the most rewarding days of my junior year. I had asked my math teacher to write a letter of recommendation at the advice of my guidance counselor. At first I was hesitant to ask him because I really struggled with the tests in his class. Early in the year, my average test grade had been a "C." But then one day I asked my teacher if he could help me after school. We agreed to a time, and he got out an old test and showed me where I had gone wrong. He then sat with me as I re-did my calculations. I saw that I did know how to do the work, I just needed to slow down so that I didn't make careless errors. I admitted to him that I had always been intimidated by math, it wasn't something that came easy to me and my approach to my tests was often to get them over with. He told me that he felt my mindset of believing I wasn't any good at math was holding me back. Following that day, we met two or three other times, and my confidence in my math ability began to grow. Over time, I started to earn high "Bs" on my math tests. My math teacher told me that he would be honored to write my letter because he rarely sees a student work as hard to turn something around as I did. He told me that he appreciated my honesty in talking with him. He also said that he felt I was a model student, and that if all students put in the time and effort that I did, that his job would be easy. I am so glad I listened to my counselor and asked my math teacher. I feel that his letter is going to represent me in a good light!

Next, the form will ask who the teacher is and in what course or courses they taught you, and often they ask for how long the teacher has known you.

Tip #3—It is best to ask a teacher who has taught you a full year. So most students ask junior year teachers, and they ask them to write the letter at the END of junior year. This way it is ready at the beginning of senior year. Many students make the mistake of asking a senior year teacher in the fall of the senior year. When the teacher has to respond that he has only taught you say eight weeks, you could see how that letter would be given less weight than a teacher who has known you for a full school year. That being said, sometimes students get a teacher senior year whom they had in a prior year, say 9th or 10th grade. In this case, this kind of letter may work out since the teacher taught you for a full year and has now reconnected with you as a senior.

Tip #4—Don't assume that you have to ask an "AP" or honors level teacher. Sometimes these teachers are asked to write many recommendations. As you might imagine, if teachers have 70 recommendations to write, they have less time to write an individual letter than a teacher who might have just 10 to write. Letters of recommendation are written on a teacher's personal time, and it is hard for a teacher to make one student sound different from another if they are writing many letters each year.

Tip #5—A letter from a foreign language teacher can actually really stand out in a stack of letters written mainly by English, history, math, or science teachers. Many students drop learning a foreign language early, so a student who chooses to stick with foreign language and excels in it may receive additional attention by the admissions officers.

A letter of recommendation is either an opportunity to gain some brownie points or not really gain anything at all. Because you want to maximize your chance of being admitted to your schools of choice, understanding the recommendation process and obtaining the best possible recommendations can help you reach your goal!

4.2: What Does the Recommendation Form Ask?

Most recommendation forms are more complex than students realize. The form doesn't just ask the teacher to write a letter (though some forms are in fact that simple). Most forms ask a teacher to rate the student on a number of factors. This is the part most students are shocked to learn about.

The form actually asks the teacher to rate the student on these factors and in relation to their peers, selecting from checkboxes that range from "below average" all the way up to "one of the top few I have encountered in my career." In between ranges from simply "average" to "outstanding." Let's take a look at some of these factors and what they mean.

Academic achievement: This addresses your overall academic accomplishments in the class. Was your grade strong across the board? Maybe it was up and down, being high on homework or report writing and low on tests, or the reverse pattern might have been true.

Intellectual promise: This refers to how the teacher views your potential—which could be quite different than your actual performance. Sometimes a teacher feels the student has a good deal of talent that has yet to be displayed, and perhaps at other times a teacher may feel the student has already stretched himself and has reached his potential.

Quality of writing: Writing is an important skill regardless of what you plan to study in college. Being able to communicate in a clear, concise, and focused manner is considered an important skill to college success. The teacher will consider whether the student's writing remained on topic and is accurate.

Creative, original thought: Some classes allow a student to display this type of skill more than others. Where assignments, labs, or problem solving allow, teachers are looking to see if the student simply follows the textbook model or whether he shows some initiative in taking what he learned and going a step further.

Productive class discussion: Some students are quieter than others; however, all students should find a way to get involved in at least some discussions. Many students are envious of that other student who is always talking in class. It surprises them to learn that sometimes those students are viewed as domineering and bossy, not giving others a chance to talk or contribute to the discussion. All students should try to strike a balance of listening well to others and then chiming in when they have something to contribute. For a student who is painfully shy, consider approaching the teacher after class to share that it feels hard to speak up, but that you had the following thoughts about the discussion. Teachers really appreciate when a student takes the time to talk to them.

Disciplined work habits: Students are often surprised to realize that teachers have their ways of observing this factor, even though this is a skill most often practiced outside of class. In the classroom, the teacher will notice if students consistently make use of class time set aside to work. Will students get started on the homework or project, or will they use this time to be chatty with friends? Teachers notice if you consistently turn in your paper the day it is due, a few days early, or a few days late. Teachers notice if worksheets have soda or coffee spilled on them, are crumpled, or covered in poor handwriting and eraser marks. Teachers notice if you ask for help before you have a problem or after disaster has struck.

Maturity: Teachers notice whether students are focused and concerned about their achievement and that of others, or whether they are mean to or uncooperative with others. Teachers hear from the substitute about students who stepped up and helped out or students who made the sub's job harder.

Motivation: Teachers notice whether students care about their work and whether they approach it with enthusiasm or dread. Teachers notice whether students are dissatisfied with a grade and ask about how they can improve. Teachers notice if students ask for clarification to be sure they are on the right track.

Leadership: Teachers notice if students volunteer to take on a leadership role, and they notice how a student carries out that leadership role whether it has been assigned to them or they volunteered for it. Do students treat all group members fairly? Do students hold all group members accountable? Do students have good project management skills, keeping the group on track?

Integrity: Do students follow the rules? If students observe others doing wrong, did they do something about it? If students make a mistake, do they own it?

Reaction to setbacks: How do students handle it when they receive a poor grade on a test or project? Do students sulk? Or do the students approach the teacher to ask where things went wrong? Do the students try harder the next time or do they give up?

Concern for others: Do the students genuinely care about their class-mates? Do they share notes with a peer who was absent? Do they stand up for a student who is getting picked on during a class debate?

Self-confidence: Can a student state his opinion, whether it is the popular opinion or not, and without wavering if someone challenges him? Does the student have his own sense of style and voice in his writing and interactions with others? Would the student stand up for someone who was being picked on?

Initiative, independence: Can the student get started on classwork with minimal direction from the teacher? Does the student pursue learning a topic he is interested in beyond the class material assigned?

Respect accorded by faculty: Is the teacher aware that the student is liked and respected by prior teachers or other teachers and administrators in the school?

Respect accorded by peers: Do other students in the school like the student? Not in a "popularity" sense, but in the sense that "this is a nice person who branches out and has friends or associates with others in different circles." Is the student known for being himself?

YOUR TURN 4.1

So How Do I Stack Up?

Directions: Now you have some insight into how teachers are considering you as a student as they complete a recommendation. It would be a good time to reflect on how you feel YOU would be rated.

- Make a list of the characteristics that you feel you have displayed or mastered well. Give an example or two of how you think you show these characteristics in the classroom and in the school community.

- Make a list of the characteristics where you feel you need to do some work. Think of some ways that you can work on those. Challenge yourself to make a conscious effort to improve.

- Ask a parent, friend, or mentor to go through the form with you and see if they made observations similar to yours. Sometimes we don't always objectively see where we shine or where we need to do some work!

4.3: Some Additional Thoughts on the Process

Don't assume that the smartest students get the best recommendations. Just because students earn good grades doesn't mean they are good classroom and community citizens. Likewise, students who struggle to earn a good grade might receive a strong recommendation because the teacher sees them working really hard to overcome challenges.

Don't think you shouldn't ask a teacher if you didn't get an "A" in the course. Earning an "A" doesn't make you a perfect student. As you have read, there are many factors a teacher considers when writing a letter. Admissions officials want to admit students who are going to stick with it when things get challenging. If a teacher can attest to how you have worked through challenges and tried your best, you may sound just like a candidate a college would want to admit!

Teachers are always watching and listening, and they may notice little things that you don't realize. For example, in the few minutes as students change classes, teachers notice behavior in the hallway, they overhear conversations, some good ones and others that contain material that they find shocking or disappointing. Teachers see students in the cafeteria. They notice who extends a seat to the new kid or the kid who is alone. They notice who bumps the tray out of someone else's hand. Teachers go to sporting events, school dances, academic competitions, concerts, and plays, and they notice students and what they are up to. Be your best self whether you think someone is watching you or not!

4.4: How Do You Ask and When Do You Do It?

Many students and parents are surprised to learn that the college admissions process occurs much earlier in senior year than they realized. Many state and private universities have rolling admissions, and it would not be unheard of for students to submit applications in late September and early October for those schools! Also Early Action and Early Decision deadlines can be as early as October 15th but more typically November 1st or 15th. Of course, there are still plenty of schools with January 1st deadlines, but since you may not know which deadlines you will have to make in your senior year, you can see how it would be advantageous to ask teachers to write their letters in the late spring of junior year, rather than waiting until the fall of senior year.

Tip #1—Please ask your teacher *in person* if they would be willing to write a recommendation for you. Many students send the teacher an email making the request, and some have even just had the recommendation form sent electronically without ever having asked the teacher. Teachers are quite dismayed when this happens. A letter of recommendation is personal and vouches for your character and achievement. Unless a teacher is unavailable because he has moved or is on some sort of leave, asking the teacher in person is a must.

Tip #2—Once the teacher has agreed to write the letter, provide the teacher with some helpful information to work with or consider while writing the letter. Students sometimes forget that teachers are teaching 100 or more students, and as much as the teacher may like you, he would appreciate having some handy information when sitting down to write your letter.

Tip #3—Remember to say please and thank you. Teachers will tell you it is a rare student who sends a thank-you note acknowledging the personal time the teacher has put into writing the letter. As will be discussed in Chapter 7, you never know when you might need something again from someone who has already done you a favor!

YOUR TURN 4.2

Preparing To Ask For A Letter

Directions: Teachers are often asked to write many recommendations each year. It is very helpful to them to have some information from you to assist them in the process. Consider typing up the answers to the below questions and providing them to the teacher.

1. Why did you select that particular teacher to write your letter? (What do you like about your experience/relationship with him or her?)

2. Give a sample list of the universities you intend to apply to (you can mention the list is still under construction).

3. If you have a good idea of what you want to study, share that. If you are undecided, mention a few areas of interest.

4. What is one way you feel you excelled in this class?

5. What is something you struggled with in this class? What actions did you take to improve?

6. What was a valuable piece of advice that this teacher offered that you benefited from? (This can be either directly to you or something that was shared with the whole class, perhaps a new method to study for their tests or a method to use in revising your writing, etc.)

7. Were there any challenges you faced outside the classroom that may have impacted you inside the classroom? There may not be anything. Or you may have had multiple absences leading up to having your tonsils removed or your parents may have been going through a divorce.

8. Provide the teacher with a brief list of school or community activities you participate in outside their classroom. This gives them a sense of how much time you had to dedicate to this class in comparison to your involvement in other activities. You cannot assume that he knows about the other things you participate in.

9. Is there anything specific you wish to have highlighted about your time in this class and/or yourself as a person?

4.5: The Take Away

- Students should understand how the recommendation process works earlier in their high school experience rather than later.

- Be aware of how others perceive you, your behavior, and your actions.

- Consciously work to build relationships with teachers so that it becomes a natural process for you.

- Remember that admissions officers prefer to hear from 11th grade teachers when possible.

- Be sure to ask the teacher in person if he is willing to write a letter for you.

- Prepare an information sheet to give to the recommendation writer to assist in writing the recommendation.

- Remember to write a thank-you note to anyone who takes the time to write a recommendation!

PREPARING A RÉSUMÉ AND COVER LETTER

hances are you've heard the word résumé many times before. You may have some idea of what a résumé is, but now you need one, and you don't know where to start! While many people think of the word résumé as something that "grown-ups" need when they are applying for a job, there are actually many reasons why you might need a résumé during high school and college. Of course you will also likely need one when you are applying for a job in the real world! But let's start with the kind you might need while you are a student!

Why might you need a résumé while a student?
- You are applying for a part-time job
- You are applying for an unpaid internship or some kind of job shadow experience
- The teacher or school counselor you ask for a recommendation asks you for one

- A college or university you are applying to requires one in the application process
- You have heard an admissions counselor or a local alumni representative of a university would appreciate one to look at during your interview
- You are applying to a trade school
- You are applying for a full-time job directly out of high school

VOICES FROM CAMPUS 5.1

A Résumé Can Help You Get A Stronger Recommendation…

So my teacher asked me to give her a résumé if I wanted her to write me a letter of recommendation. I told her, "Sure no problem." But then I walked away and freaked out. Résumé? I don't have a résumé! I've never had a job, so I am not sure what I am supposed to give her! But then I went and talked to my guidance counselor, and she told me that you don't have to have job experience to prepare a résumé. A résumé is about communicating the skills that I have, as well as other general information such as my GPA, my contact information, and my hobbies. She then showed me a computer program that helped me build a résumé that included everything I do. I asked my mom to look it over, and she reminded me about a couple of volunteer experiences I had done earlier in high school that I had forgotten about, so I included those too. When I gave it to my teacher, she said it would be a big help in writing her letter! In the end, I am glad I have a résumé going because my guidance counselor told me I might need one for my college applications anyway!

5.1: What Is a Résumé?

It is a typed document, often just one page, which communicates a number of vital pieces of information about who you are and what skills you have. If you are young and don't have a lot of work experience, don't worry. You can still prepare a résumé that can be effective. Obviously, as you grow older and you have more experience, you will have more to put on a résumé.

5.2: The Résumé:
For High School, a Part-time Job, or College

But before we start, here are some tips to consider when building a résumé for use during high school or when applying for a part-time job or college admission:

- The résumé must be typed. While it is often amusing to use fun or fancy fonts and colors while posting on Facebook or Instagram, it is best to keep a résumé in a standard/traditional font that is easy to read, such as Times New Roman. A 12-point font is usually standard, along with one-inch margins.

- Be sure to use spell and grammar check on your résumé. Even after you have done that, it is often best to ask a trustworthy adult to review it, because unfortunately sometimes grammar and spell check miss errors! Given the large numbers of résumés that are received, those with errors will usually get eliminated immediately.

- Make a list of all the things you have done during high school. In and out of school activities count. Typically a college admissions counselor, an employer or interviewer will want to know about things you've done during high school and not before then, but sometimes earlier life experience can count. For example, if you've taken piano or violin lessons since you were in first grade, that shows a long-standing commitment and the depth of your experience. So you might list something like the fact that you have played piano for 10 years starting in elementary school, versus listing that you attended a Cub Scouts camp during the summer of fifth grade, which would be less relevant since it happened one time and a while ago.

- Be sure you are honest. Do not make things up or greatly embellish things you've done or participated in, because admissions officers have a good gauge on what high school students are capable of.

5.3: The Résumé: For Job Applications

If you have finished high school and are now applying for a full-time job or applying for a job following college, here are some additional tips beyond the ones already listed:

- Include keywords that résumé filters look for. Ask someone with experience in your major or area of employment to review your résumé for those words or phrases so that you know what they are.

- Don't exaggerate! Some employers avoid those résumés where candidates have obviously embellished their responsibilities by using euphemisms or words that overly complicate the work they did, because these people tend to overcomplicate other things as well. In addition, the reader of your résumé will often follow up and verify given information.

5.4: No Work Experience! What Do I Do?

The best way to build a résumé before you have work experience is to have life experience. If you've never worked a job with a paycheck, that is okay. You can still build a résumé. Think about the things you do in your everyday life. If you are involved in school or community clubs, sports, organizations, or childcare, you have life experience with which to work.

Here are some examples to think about:

Babysitting (paid or unpaid): Maybe you watch your younger siblings until Mom or Dad are home from work. The kind of skills that are involved include patience, maturity, ability to manage or be responsible for one or more children, creativity (do you plan activities?), meal preparation (do you prepare snacks, lunch, or dinner?), tutoring (might you help them with homework?), or spur-of-the-moment decision making.

Landscaping (paid or unpaid): Maybe you maintain a regular time commitment to mow your lawn, or do you have a small business mowing neighbors' lawns? Do you weed and mulch flower beds? Do you help dig in plants, shrubs, and/or trees or care for a neighbor's yard when they are on vacation? Skills involved could include responsibility to a weekly commitment and time management (if you mow multiple lawns). If you mow for others, do you prepare invoices to collect money? Maintenance of equipment, such as caring for the mower or other tools, is a good life skill to have.

Sports: Do you belong to a local community-, travel-, or school-based team? Regardless of the sport, you have learned skills. If you play a team sport, you have learned teamwork. You have made a commitment to practice and improve skills. If you've received any awards like Most Improved Player, Most Valuable Player, or have been named a captain, this shows leadership. You may have a set responsibility on the team, such as leading warm-ups, bringing the water bottles, or bringing certain equipment. You may have had to do fundraising to purchase new equipment or to cover costs for traveling to tournaments. If you play an individual sport, you have again made a time commitment, completed practices, workshops, or camps to improve upon your skills, and you may have won some recognition through competition or results.

School-Based Clubs: There are many school clubs and organizations. These are just some examples: the yearbook; the school paper; Future Business Leaders of America; Black Student Union; National Honors Society; a foreign language–based honor society; academic teams; specialty interest groups like skiing, fishing, or the arts. In these clubs, you have again made a time commitment, and you may responsible for something, perhaps writing articles, being a photographer, or preparing for a competition.

Acting/Plays/Musicals: Typically, the time commitment to prepare for a play or musical is extensive (10 or more hours a week). Be sure to list what role you had, such as a lead, being in the chorus, stage crew, or publicity. If you've helped with any "behind the scenes" activities like stage props, costumes, lighting, sound, make-up, or directing, all of these are significant and important contributions!

Music (Singing or Instrumental): Participating in choir, band, orchestra, jazz band, or other musical groups in and out of school are activities that many admissions officers and employers are interested in seeing. Taking a weekly lesson for voice instruction or on your instrument, playing at church or a coffee house, or having your own band are all items that should be listed.

Leadership (for example, student council/class officers, homeroom representative, junior scout master, camp counselor, captain of a team): Many admissions counselors will talk about wanting to see leadership, so getting involved in student council, scouting organizations, or something similar in your religious organization are great ways to learn and demonstrate leadership skills. When you are involved in these kinds of activities, it usually means having to work with groups or teams of students, representing others fairly, reporting important information to your community, and sometimes even having to manage a budget or fund of money. All of these things show great responsibility on your part!

Other Outside-of-School Clubs: Many students belong to clubs in the community that are not associated with school, and they don't realize that when applying to college or a job, all activities count. If you have taken a course in first aid or in emergency response and have a special certification as a result, this counts. Participation in something through your YMCA, Girl or Boy Scouts, or the Rotary Club also counts and should also be listed.

Religious Education: Participating in weekly Sunday school, youth group, Hebrew school, and other religious activities such as the choir or being an assistant to a Sunday school teacher are quality activities that should be listed.

Volunteer Work: Some students collect food for the local food pantry or help with holiday toy drives, while others volunteer as a candy striper at the local hospital. Some students participate in 5k runs to raise money or volunteer at the local Ronald McDonald house. There are many different volunteer activities out there. Some students do multiple one-time volunteer activities and feel these activities cannot be listed because each of them occurred just once. The way to address this is to make a general category called volunteer activities and then list all the 5k runs or the different food pantries for which you've collected food.

Special Summer Programs: Many students do different kinds of activities over the summer. You may go on an outdoor exploratory camp week, or you might be a counselor-in-training at the sleepaway camp you grew up going to. You might go to a college or university campus and participate in training for a specific sport, or you might go to a university and take a one-, two-, or three-week summer course or program. You might travel to another country with a school or community group or go on a church mission or Habitat for Humanity build. All of these can be listed as summer-based activities!

Hobbies: If you sew, garden, make movies, fly-fish, have logged in the hours and obtained your scuba or pilot's license, or do anything else where you have dedicated yourself to learning or practicing something, you can list it!

Paid Work Experience: Many students do have paid work experience at a relatively young age. This can include babysitting, lawn mowing, bussing tables at a local restaurant, or working at a carwash. Due to the legalities of child labor laws, there are many jobs that students cannot obtain until they are 16 or older, and admissions counselors and employers realize the amount of job experience a younger student can have is limited!

This is not an all-inclusive list, as there may be things that you do that are not listed here. A general rule of thumb is if it involves a time commitment and effort on your part, it can be included on the résumé. If you are not involved in much, now might be a good time to reflect on all the things available in the world to get involved in and pick a couple or more things you can manage! Your résumé may have a strong impact on the kind of college or university you are admitted to or the kind of job you eventually obtain. You will constantly be building a résumé throughout your high school and college years. If you choose an alternative path after high school other than college, your résumé may actually impact employment opportunities sooner than later.

YOUR TURN 5.1

Preparing To Make Your Own Résumé

Directions: Keep track of the below information so you have it when you need it.

1. Write your name, address, phone number, and email address at the top of the page. Then list some other information that would be helpful such as the name of the high school you attend, what grade you are currently in, and what year you will graduate. If you feel it could be relevant, you can even list your GPA. If you've taken challenging courses such as honors, AP, or IB courses, you could list those. If you are applying for a job where you have already taken some relevant coursework, such as woodworking, computer graphic design, web development, etc., you could have a section called "Relevant Coursework."

2. Write down the kinds of activities, clubs, sports, religious participation you have done during high school. It might be good to create categories such as the ones just listed.

3. Now for each activity, think of two or three (or more if there are more) skills or accomplishments you have gained from participating in the activity. If you have had a leadership or organizational role, be sure to highlight this.

5.5: Making a Simple Résumé for Use During High School

There are a number of reasons why you might need a résumé during high school, such as for a job interview, in order to obtain a recommendation from a teacher, or for your college applications and interviews. There are many different styles of résumés. Overall, unless you are applying to a job or to a college or university that provides very specific directions about what it needs to look like, you can design one that best represents you. Some students have done a lot, and others have less life experience to work with. Several different résumé styles and examples have been provided to give you some models to work with.

YOUR TURN 5.2

Making Your Own Résumé Made Simple

Directions: There are several different résumé styles provided here. Take a look at each one and figure out which one might be the best style for you to utilize given the amount of experience you have to share. Then create your own following one of the styles or even combining different aspects of the styles to suit your needs.

Style #1—This style works well for a student who hasn't done a ton of extracurricular activities because it spreads everything out and makes the page look full. This is a great style to use for either a college application or to provide to a potential recommendation writer.

Activity Résumé
Student's First and Last Name

Activity Name:	Hours per week/season	Position
9th grade:		
Freshman Soccer	10 hours/week	Center Forward
Winter Track	10 hours/week	Sprinter
Boy Scouts	2 hours/week	Member Troop #52
10th grade:		
JV Soccer	10 hours/week	Center Forward
Student Council	1 hour/week	Homeroom Representative
Winter Track	10 hours/week	Sprinter
*UNITY	1 hr/week	Member
Summer:		
Camp Arrowhead	40 hours/6 weeks	Counselor-In-Training
11th grade:		
Varsity Soccer	10 hours/week	Halfback
Giant's Supermarket	12 hours/week	Cashier
*UNITY	1 hr/week	Member
Summer:		
Penn State Soccer Intensive Full week overnight program		
12th grade:		
Varsity Soccer	10 hours/week	Halfback
Travel Soccer	10 hours/week (year round)	Halfback
Giant's Supermarket	12 hours/week	Cashier
*UNITY	1 hr/week	Member

While many activities are clear and obvious, some clubs or groups may be unknown to the majority, and in these instances, you can define the group at the bottom of the page, like below:

*UNITY is a group that mentors new students. I serve as a host to help new students adjust and become a part of the new school community.

Style #2—This résumé style works well for a student who is applying to college and has engaged in a variety of different activities and needs more space to work with.

Résumé

Your Name:Street Address:
City, State, Zip:
Telephone:
Email:

School Attended:
Cumulative GPA:

School Activities:	Varsity Tennis – 9, 11
	Junior Varsity Track – 10
	Key Club – 9, 11
	Finance Club – 11
Community Activities:	CYO Basketball – 9, 10, 11
	Guitar (Individual and Band) – 9, 10, 11
	Recreational/Pickup Sports – 9, 10, 11
Service to Others:	AID for Friends (meals for elderly and homeless) – 10, 11
	Miscellaneous Community Service (raking leaves) – 9, 10, 11
	Coached Middle School Basketball Team – 11
Summer Experiences:	Worked at Picket Post Swim & Tennis Club (4 Years)
	Family Trips to Aruba, North Carolina, Cayman Islands (Winter)
	Numerous Trips to New Jersey Shore
Employment History:	Picket Post Swim & Tennis Club (4 years)
	Tennis Monitor (2 years)
	Lifeguard (2 years)
	Babysitter (4 years)
Honors & Awards:	Selected to represent my high school in a summit meeting with other area high schools
	Various Athletic Awards – 9, 10, 11
	Honor Roll – 9, 10, 11

Style #3—This style works well for a student who has worked a couple or more jobs or internships and is often used when applying for a full-time job or graduate school.

Name

Address

Phone and Email

EDUCATION:

Name of university, location, year of anticipated graduation

Major: Name of Major   **Minor:** (if you had one)

GPA: you can list overall cumulative GPA   **Major GPA:** if you have one

Dissertation: brief description (or honors thesis or special project if you did one)

Study Abroad: if you went abroad, list name of country or university and semester of the program

Relevant Coursework: list courses you took that relate to the job requirements

Objective: To obtain a position doing or utilizing (then provide a brief summary of the job you are trying to obtain)

PROFESSIONAL EXPERIENCE

Job or Internship Title, location (city and state)   Year

- List one responsibility
- List another responsibility
- List another responsibility

Job or Internship Title, location (city and state)   Year

- List one responsibility
- List another responsibility
- List another responsibility

ADDITIONAL INFORMATION: List hobbies, special skills or talents, or clubs or groups you belong to.

5.6: What Is a Cover Letter, and What Do I Put in It?

A cover letter is typically a brief written statement that would accompany your résumé. The cover letter should introduce you and should be customized to what you are applying for, whether that is to a specific college or a specific job. Oftentimes you won't need one. For example, if your teachers ask for a résumé in order to help them write your recommendation or if you are meeting with an interviewer at a college, you would not need a cover letter. However, if you are mailing, faxing, or emailing your résumé to an individual or corporation in response to an ad seeking applicants, then a cover letter is often a great idea. Sometimes a job advertisement will state that a résumé *and* cover letter are required. Through a cover letter you can offer a brief explanation about who you are and why you see yourself as a good fit for that particular job or opportunity. A cover letter is an opportunity to differentiate yourself from the dozens of other applicants by being able to point out a thing or two about yourself that you would otherwise only get to do if you are selected for an interview. Preparing a cover letter shows that you care enough to go the extra mile.

You have given the composition of your email or cover letter great thought and are now happy with the results. It's clear, concise, and error free. However, how you end your letter is just as important as the content. Any written communication needs a closing and a signature (your full name for initial communications). When you are deciding how best to close a letter, it's a good idea to consider the context of the letter and to whom it is going. What works for a friend or colleague may not work for someone you have never met when applying for a job. Here are some closings that you might want to consider:[i]

For most interactions (including that with a teacher, professor, or college admissions counselor): Consider using "Sincerely." Sincerely conveys the right tone for formal correspondence, such as a cover letter.

For formal business interaction: Consider using the ending "Regards." This works in professional emails precisely because there's nothing unexpected or remarkable about it.

If you've made a request in the cover letter: Consider saying a simple "thank you" or "thanks in advance." According to the Boomerang study,

---

[i] Hertzberg, K. "How to End an Email: 9 Never-Fail Sign-Offs and 9 to Avoid." *Grammarly Blog.* 2 June 2017. Web. https://www.grammarly.com/blog/how-to-end-an-email/

emails that include *thanks in advance* have the highest response rate. You're saying that you'll be grateful when (not if) the person you're emailing follows up. In more formal circumstances, thanking someone in advance may come across as too demanding, so be sure to think through whether it is wise to be making the request. It seems that most of the time a simple "thank you" is the way to go.

Expressing gratitude: There's never really a wrong time to express appreciation when someone has helped you out. "I appreciate your [help, input, feedback, etc.]" is a terrific expression to consider when thanking someone for any help they have offered or provided.

VOICES FROM CAMPUS 5.2

Mackenzie...

Mackenzie: I am so excited! I just received a call that I got the summer job I applied to a few weeks ago!

Mackenzie's mom: That's great news, Mackenzie!

Mackenzie: When I showed up for the interview, the store manager told me that I had been selected for an interview because my cover letter was really strong. She said I showed how I was a good fit for the job.

Mackenzie's mom: What did you say in your letter?

Mackenzie: I told them I had been shopping there for years and why their clothes really fit my personality. I shared that many of my friends had started wearing their clothes as a result of me always raving about their style and quality. I also mentioned that I had experience working at a different store last summer, so I knew a bit about customer service, keeping the store in a presentable fashion, as well as how to work a cash register. I also said that I was always on time, reliable, and that I had only missed one week of work all last summer due to our family vacation.

5.7: Extra Tips for Making a Résumé for Graduate School or the Job Market

Admissions personnel, recruiters, and employers will tell any candidate that you cannot have one résumé and use it to apply to many different schools or jobs. Applicants can do themselves a huge favor by ensuring they clearly connect their experience with the aspects of the graduate program they are applying to or responsibilities of the job they are hoping to land.

For Graduate School

When you apply to graduate school, you are applying to a very specific program, not just for general admission to a school as when you applied for an undergraduate degree. Each graduate department within a university has a specific philosophy, and sometimes specialty areas within a larger program. You must carefully research each program you are applying to, looking to learn about the professors in that department, their philosophy and academic and research interests. Then you must demonstrate how the undergraduate coursework and internship(s) you participated in have prepared you to enter that program. If, during this process, you realize that you may not have taken the relevant background coursework or done any internships that are relevant to that graduate program, you may decide it is best to take a year off from applying while taking those relevant courses and doing either a paid or unpaid internship or research, thus increasing your odds of admission. Graduate school applications can cost $200 or more each, so you want to be sure you have a good chance of being admitted before haphazardly applying! It might even be a good idea to meet with professors or coordinators of the programs that you are interested in to learn what kind of candidate they are looking for in their graduate students. This way you can formulate a plan that makes you an attractive candidate for that program.

For a Job

One way to highlight your fit for the position is to add a *very* brief overview at the top of your résumé called an "objective" or "summary" that calls out a few of your relevant key skills. You can also use LinkedIn or other online resources to look at current employees in the same role or department to which you're applying and customize your résumé based on what you discover about people currently in that job or on that team. Most big companies with recruiting departments review every résumé they receive. The résumés that generally get passed to hiring managers are those that clearly fit the requirements of the job posting. They look for keywords and matches between the skills that the hiring manager needs and what the candidate has on her résumé. For example, if the job is analytical, emphasize your analytical skills and accomplishments, highlighting academic coursework relevant to the job or internship experience gained during your college years. If the job is sales or marketing oriented, find ways to emphasize your strong social and communication skills, as well as any and all experiences where you've sold or promoted something.

In addition, craft the résumé so that skills and contributions support why you are the ideal candidate for the job. Include things like:

- Evidence of follow-through
- Ability to work independently
- Strong social skills and team player—ability to work in a team setting
- Leadership skills
- Analytical skills
- Proficiency in Microsoft Office (Excel, Word, PowerPoint, etc.)
- Good communication skills
- Willing to go the distance to achieve a successful outcome

Some might wonder whether having different résumés would be considered cheating or lying. It is not cheating or lying if the skills and courses you highlight are factual. When you apply to one job, you might highlight the coursework from your major. While applying to another job, the coursework from your minor might be more relevant. When you work at a job or internship, you gain many skills, not just one, so when you look at a job description, you might decide to emphasize one skill set gained through a job over another.

Getting your résumé to stand out from all the others will take some creativity, due diligence, and attention to detail. Now is not the time to blast out dozens of one-size-fits-all résumés. Now is the time to customize, because the effort you put in will likely lead to the amount of opportunities that will come your way. You will need to package your experiences and interests in your cover letter and résumé in ways that target specific opportunities.

5.8: The Take Away

- A résumé is a vital document that you will need for many reasons, ranging from obtaining a letter of recommendation, to applying to a part- or full-time job, to applying to college or graduate school.

- You don't need paid work experience to make a résumé. You can build a great résumé using life experience.

- Be sure to carefully edit your résumé looking for any errors, and seek feedback from an objective person.

- Customize your résumé to the opportunity you are going after (graduate school, full- or part-time job).

- Send a customized cover letter with your résumé when appropriate.

Online Resource:

https://www.résumé-now.com/builder/rbdesktop/edit-résumé.aspx

This site offers a variety of résumé templates. You can choose the one you like the most, and it helps you build your own for free!

THE INTERVIEW— COLLEGE, GRADUATE SCHOOL, OR THE JOB MARKET

6.1: Preparing for a Successful Interview

As you have grown older throughout your school years, you probably became aware that at some point or another you would need to participate in an interview. You might need to be interviewed for a part-time job, an internship, during the college admissions process, and almost certainly when looking for full-time employment. It would probably ease your mind to know what to expect: how you should dress, what you might be asked, and how to follow up with your interviewer. Being a good communicator is essential to having a successful interview.

6.2: How Can I Get Ready?

Reading this chapter carefully and preparing and practicing for the interview with a neutral person such as an older sibling, parent, teacher, guidance counselor, or mentor is a great way to start. The majority of advice offered here applies to all interviewing scenarios. However, there will be times where advice will be labeled as specific to a certain type of interview. For any interview, try to go to bed early the night before so that you are hopefully better rested and more relaxed in the morning. Allow plenty of time to arrive at your interview destination. If you haven't been to the location before, you might want to familiarize yourself with the area in advance so that you don't get lost and cause yourself additional stress on the day of the actual interview!

How you should dress depends on the kind of interview it is. If you are meeting with a neighbor down the street to discuss whether you'd be a good fit as the family babysitter, you can dress more casually than if you are interviewing with a college admissions counselor. Of course, the first rule of thumb is to be neat and clean. Your hair should be tidy and not hanging too much over your face, especially your eyes (you don't want to appear to be hiding behind your hair)! Your clothes should be clean and wrinkle free. For a casual interview, what you would wear to school for a nice event would be fine, but if you are interviewing for a job shadow or internship or for college admissions, you should wear something dressier. For females, this doesn't mean you have to wear a dress or skirt if that is absolutely not your style. In that case, dress pants and a nice blouse or sweater would be good. If you do wear a dress or skirt, be sure that it isn't too short—no shorter than two inches above the knee is a good rule of thumb to follow. You always want to err on the side of being conservative. If you are male and it is a more casual situation, dress pants and a collared shirt are often fine. In a more formal situation, suit pants and a dress shirt work well. A tie or blazer is often not required, though if you enjoy wearing either, you should feel free! If you are interviewing with an admissions counselor, you might want to check the admissions website for that particular college or university, as oftentimes there is advice about how to dress for the interview. Most admissions sites and counselors encourage students to dress "neat and clean" but usually state that a suit is not required. If you feel unsure of how to dress, check in with a trusted adult, like your guidance counselor!

An Interview May Not Always Be Formal and Fancy...

I was so glad that I went on the website for the university I was about to visit. I had just had an argument with my mom over what I should wear. She said that when she did interviews at my age she wore a skirt suit. I thought that sounded way too fancy. On the admissions page for the website, it said to dress casually in a neat clean outfit. When I arrived for my interview, all the other students in the waiting area were also dressed casually. I would have felt very uncomfortable and embarrassed if I had been overdressed!

6.3: What to Have and Not Have With You

Oftentimes, you don't need to bring anything with you but your smile. However, there are some occasions where bringing a copy of your résumé may be a good idea. If you are interviewing for college admissions or a part- or full-time job, it would be good to bring a copy of your résumé with you just in case the interviewer requests it. For a college admissions interview, you might also want to have a bottle of water with you. Carrying a bottle of water with you is not considered unusual or rude, and you can actually use the bottle of water to help buy you a few seconds to think if you need a moment after you are asked a question. You can always take a sip of water while gathering your thoughts! What you don't want to bring with you is a hot cup of coffee or tea, because if you are nervous and you spill it on yourself or someone else, that would create stress for all! Also, do not have your cell phone out or in your hands. You can have your cell phone in a purse or in your pocket, but it must be turned off—that means completely off. There is nothing like a vibrating cell phone to interrupt a conversation and to potentially annoy your interviewer, leaving him with a bad impression of you!

6.4: What Will I Be Asked?

The kinds of questions you will be asked will vary depending on the purpose of the interview. Obviously you cannot predict every question you will be asked, but it would be a great idea to have thought through some of the questions you may be asked. It is also important to understand why you are being asked certain questions and what the interviewer is hoping to learn about you from your answers.

Below are common questions broken down by category. The questions are likely to be asked of a high school student applying for part-time work or for college admissions.

Getting to Know You

1. Tell me a bit about yourself. Yikes—this is a very open-ended question, and you could answer it in any number of ways. You could state your age, grade, and what school you attend. You could share where you live and if you've always lived there. You could list whether you have siblings or if you live with one or both parents, a grandparent, or guardian. You could share some fun fact about yourself, perhaps something you enjoy doing in your spare time, such as reading, a particular kind of exercise, sport, or travel. If you are interviewing for a full-time job right out of high school or college, you might also mention when you will be graduating.

2. What brings you here? You should have some reasons for why you are at that specific school (or part-time job) and they should not be generic, such as "Because you have a great reputation." Anyone can give that answer easily. They want to see you have done some homework on why the school or part-time job is a good fit for you. These can be reasons like a particular major they offer, a certain professor you want to study under, particular clubs or groups they have that you plan to participate in, etc. In the case of part-time work, the answer could be because you are looking to gain more responsibility and some income and would like to do that in a place you feel you'd be happy working!

3. What are your greatest strengths? (This question may be asked in single or plural form, meaning they may ask for just one strength or

they may allow you to share more than one.) You should of course have at least one in mind and be able to offer a reason as to why it is a strength!

4. What is your greatest weakness? (This question may be asked in single or plural form.) Everyone has weaknesses. Being able to address something that is hard or a challenge for you is expected. While honesty is important, you may want to think about your various weaknesses and think of the one that doesn't create too much concern. For example, it may not be best to admit you do things at the last minute, even if you do. Overall, getting things done on time is important to one's success as a student or employee.

5. Have you faced any particular challenges or circumstances that have had a significant impact on your life? Again, most people have faced challenges, so it is okay to share, but it is usually best to be brief and to focus more on how you came out of a situation a better person or better for the experience.

6. Do you know what you want to study? If you are undecided, please share some areas of interest. If you have a solid idea of what you want to study, do not hesitate to share, but also be prepared to share *why* you want to study that subject. If you truly don't know, be prepared to share some areas of interest and, again, *why* you have those interests.

Small-Talk Questions

Overall these are relatively harmless questions that don't have right or wrong answers but are meant to generate basic conversation.

1. What is your favorite book (or variations such as favorite movie, TV series, band)? It is best to generally avoid highly controversial or violent material.

2. What is your favorite subject? The reason the subject is your favorite is almost more important than which one. Be prepared to explain why you love the subject.

3. What is your least favorite subject? Again, there is typically not a wrong answer here. However, think this through. If you want to study engineering, it would not help you to say that science or math are your least favorite subjects since they are critical to the profession. Also be sure that you never blame a teacher in this answer. For example, it is not advisable to say, "I hated algebra because the teacher was horrible." Even if the teacher was, this answer will be a turn-off.

4. What do you do in your spare time? Again, most answers will be just fine, with the exception of "nothing." It would also be advisable to avoid something like, "I only play video games." Usually the person asking the question wants to hear several things in your answer.

5. Do you play any sports or belong to any clubs/groups? Some people could go on and on with this answer. It is best to just highlight the top two or three things and the extent of your involvement, and if they ask or allow for more, you can expand.

"Loaded" Questions—Getting at Something Specific

1. Do you read or watch the news? If so, what is your primary source of the news? Answering "no" to this question is not advisable. Most admissions counselors want to know you have some general awareness of world events and that you know reliable news sources to go to find information.

2. Did you vote in the recent election? If you are not yet 18, the answer is an easy "no." If you are 18 are older, many admissions counselors like to hear that you have registered to vote and that you have or will be voting. There are many people who feel the right to vote is one of the most important rights in the United States.

3. What do you think is the greatest issue facing the United States right now? What do you think is the greatest issue facing the world? The admissions counselors like to see that you have an awareness of what is going on in the world beyond your own household and even beyond your local community. It is important to have some idea about a couple of major national and international issues and be able to discuss what you know about them.

4. Have you ever pursued something that you learned inside the classroom in your personal life outside the classroom? Many students have not decided to pursue something beyond the classroom, but this question is often asked, especially at the more competitive universities. If you haven't decided to start reading a new genre you were exposed to in English class, or create a family tree following an interesting history lesson, or begin sketching on your own following an art class, now might be the time to think about something simple you could work on beyond the classroom!

5. Who do you most admire and why? Often the "why" part of your answer is more important. You could pick your grandmother, a major political figure, or a prominent figure in the profession you hope to enter, but have a good reason as to why you think that person is so great!

6. If you could spend one day with anyone, living or dead, who would it be and why? The formula to this is quite similar to Question 5. The reason for why you want to spend time with the person is almost more important than the "who."

7. What would you do if you saw someone do the wrong thing? You may or may not have ever found yourself in this situation, but it is important to think through how you would answer it. Of course, part of your answer should include finding a way to bring the issue to someone in a position to help resolve or address it.

8. What makes you a good match for our college/university? Be ready to go beyond generic answers like, "I am a hard worker," or "I want to graduate from a prestigious university." Be able to speak to the specifics of that university that are a good match for you (e.g., size, location, major and or minor(s) offered, special extracurricular activities, etc.).

9. Where do you see yourself five years from now? (Sometimes there will be a variation of this, such as a year from now or 10 years from now.) The interviewer is looking to see if you have thought about long-term goals in addition to short-term ones. Are you interested in going to graduate school (and if so, why)? Do you see yourself working in a particular career or location or having an impact on something?

10. Do you have any questions for me? While you might think the answer should be "no," most interviewers actually want you to ask them a question or two because it shows interest.

Some example questions would be:

- Did you attend this school? If the answer is "yes," you can ask them what they liked most about it when they were a student. If they answer "no," you can ask them what they find most special about the community they work in.

- What are the most popular things students like to do here?

- Do you feel like the professors are available to students outside the classroom?

- Are there many opportunities for students to do research or get an internship?

- What percent of the student body studies abroad?

- Any other specific question you may have that was not addressed during the interview.

YOUR TURN 6.1

Preparing For An Interview

Directions: Whether preparing for a college interview or a job interview, look at the example questions provided and then put pen to paper. Jot down some notes or points you might make for each question. You could do this in bullet point form. You don't need to write out complete sentences, and you don't want to overthink or practice too much. Doing so might increase any anxiety you are already feeling, and you may sound too rehearsed when it comes time to do the actual interview! After you have jotted down some notes for each of the questions, ask a trusted friend, adult, teacher, or counselor to ask you the questions aloud and then practice answering them. Make a note of questions you struggled with so that you can go back and spend more time later thinking about those.

6.5: Interviewing for Full-Time Employment

Some of the advice offered here is similar to that which was offered to students in high school; however, some key differences or additional details that apply to entering the full-time job market following additional training (such as college) are shared below.

Before the Interview

- Dress professionally and appropriately for the job. Often going with a suit is a good idea. Dressing on the conservative side is always a safe bet.

- Research the company and interviewers (if you've been told who they are) in advance. You should have at least a basic understanding of how the company started, what the company does, who they serve, and potentially even have some knowledge of their competitors if they have competitors. Look up the people with whom you are meeting on LinkedIn or the company's website.

- One of the best things you can do to be prepared is to practice with someone, such as the folks at the career resource center at your college, university, or training institute. Practice answering questions while making eye contact and delivering responses that answer the question you were asked. Being able to provide supporting examples to paint a picture for the interviewer of how their company/team/department will benefit from hiring you would be icing on the cake.

Typically a job interviewer will open the interview in the same manner as a college admissions counselor by asking you to share more about yourself. The candidate's response to this question is extremely revealing. Do not just restate your résumé. The interviewer is likely trying to see if you can envision yourself within the bigger picture of their organization. If you are savvy and perceptive, you will be able to speak to the benefits you will bring to the employer while also revealing a bit about who you are as a person. You must demonstrate what benefits the employer will receive from your experience, accomplishments, qualifications, and abilities. And above all, be honest.

VOICES FROM THE REAL WORLD 6.2

Insight From A Real Life Interviewer...

A person who works for a global financial firm and does a great deal of hiring shares the following true stories about interviewing candidates for positions at this prestigious firm:

"There have been a few interviews that I ended almost instantly. Once was when I caught a candidate in a lie within the first five minutes. His résumé said he graduated from 'Arizona State University, Phoenix,' which I found strange because I didn't think they had a campus there. When questioned, he folded and admitted it was University of Phoenix."

"Another time, the first question I asked a recent college grad was to tell me something about herself that I couldn't learn from her résumé. She proceeded to start reciting her résumé without taking a breath for five minutes. When I tried to interrupt, she said, 'Sorry, but I'm not done answering your question.' I told her she was done and wished her well as the interview was over.

"The most memorable was a kid who came in and immediately I knew he wouldn't make it through the interview. He wasn't wearing a tie, let alone a suit, just a dress shirt and pants. He looked like he had just woken up, and I could tell he was severely hung over as he reeked of booze. I asked him if he had a late night, he said, 'Yeah, I'm sorry.' I said, 'I am, too. Best of luck with your interviews.'"

Below is a list of other potential questions you could be asked. Most are similar to questions in the previous section, so refer back to those if you feel like you need some examples. Again, do not hesitate to use resources available to you, such as the counselors in the career center.

- What are your strengths and weaknesses?
- Where do you see yourself in five years?
- What is it about this particular company that makes you want to work here?
- What did you do in your previous jobs and how and where did you make a difference?
- What are some examples of contributions that set you apart from your co-workers?

- How do your skills prepare you for this job?
- How have you handled conflicts when they arise with co-workers? Can you give me an example?
- Do you need or prefer a lot of supervision, or do you prefer working independently once given a task?
- What are some examples of when you were given an assignment and successfully took it to completion?

In general, many candidates come to interviews having researched the company and trends in interviewing and are prepared with answers. However, the one area where many job candidates struggle is explaining what they can do, so make sure that you are prepared to present yourself, your skills, and your goals!

Consider visiting Monster.com's website for more examples of potential interview questions (https://www.monster.com/career-advice/article/100-Potential-Interview-Questions).

VOICES FROM THE REAL WORLD 6.3

Charles...

Another interview story from Charles (name changed to protect identity), owner of an engineering firm:

"A young man came in for an interview. His résumé was good but not outstanding. He had a 3.0 GPA. He was respectful and seemed knowledgeable in his field. But like I always do, I put aside the paperwork, pulled up my chair, and had a conversation with this young man. I wanted to get to know him as a person who might work for me. During our conversation, I discovered some very enlightening and life-changing information—life changing for him and our company. For four years this young man got up at 4 a.m. and worked at UPS until 8:30 a.m. He went to class and maintained a 3.0 GPA. Sure, it wasn't a 4.0. But you know what? I don't care. This man demonstrated a strong work ethic. He was able to multitask and handle life. He was putting himself through school, and he persevered for four years—maintaining a grueling schedule in order to meet his long-term goal of graduating with a degree in engineering and landing a good job. Guess what? I hired him! He is the type of person I want on my team."

There are many high school and college students who work part time, maybe even full time while going to school. Juggling work and academic schedules and responsibilities is one of those "soft skills" and character traits that will set you apart from others. If you have to do so for financial reasons or just choose to do so, don't be afraid to share this on your résumé or discuss it, as needed, at your interview. A student who works night shift every weekend demonstrates his ability to prioritize responsibilities and manage his time. It demonstrates a level of maturity and shows that you can take the challenges that life hands you.

6.6: Turning the Tables—Ask Questions, Too!

Be prepared with two or three questions for each person you meet. Whether you realize it or not, not asking questions can suggest a lack of interest to interviewers. Some possible questions might include:

- What are the qualities of the most successful people in this job? (If this question can be asked early in the interview, then the candidate can tailor their comments to fulfill these characteristics.)
- Can you describe a typical day for the person doing this job?
- What are the short-term goals for the person who earns this job?
- I believe I would be very good in this position. Is there any other information I can provide?

Being Prepared[i]

- Plan on arriving with plenty of time to spare. Not too early, not too late is the best advice. If the area is unfamiliar to you, you may want to take a trial run the day before.
- It may be best to be empty-handed (with the exception of a copy of your résumé), meaning no cell phone or beverage unless you are offered one while waiting to get started.
- Greet members of the interview committee individually with a warm smile, firm handshake, and make eye contact. Don't forget to show

[i]Hansen, R. "10 Best Job Interview Tips for Jobseekers." Quintessential LiveCareer. Web. 03 June 2017. https://www.livecareer.com/quintessential/top-10-job-interview-tips-jobseekers

appreciation to anyone with whom you come in contact. This includes the receptionist or secretary who might have gotten you a drink of water or helped arrange the interview.

- Remember the power of nonverbal communication. This is as important as what you say. Stand straight and tall. Avoid fidgeting, overuse of gestures and hand movements, crossed arms, and slouching.

- Articulate your answers in a way that is concise and answers the question. Try to avoid using the following words: "like," "um," and any other "place holders." Avoid slang. Use vocabulary that is conducive to the position for which you are applying.This next part is tricky—be humble, but confident. Do not come off as arrogant or cocky but show some degree of content knowledge.

- Remember to ask questions. You might be interested in knowing about opportunities for training or advancement. Being inquisitive can be viewed as an asset. However, a word to the wise—do not ask questions about salary, compensation packages, or any special needs. Those questions need to wait until after you have been offered the job.[ii]

[ii] Writer, Staff. "Women—12 Tips to Ace Your Job Interview." *Educate to Advance*. 3 June 2017. Web. http://www.educatetoadvance.com/women-12-tips-to-ace-your-job-interview/

VOICES FROM THE REAL WORLD 6.4

More From Charles…

And finally, Charles shares a story about one of the most impressive candidates he encountered. Someone who possessed those two important but often elusive skills—confidence and humility.

"Jacob was a 4.0 graduate of Widener University where he was a member of the track team. He had participated in an 18-week program on leadership qualities, which certainly set him apart from other candidates and I found that intriguing. As we talked, he asked so many interesting and thought-provoking questions. He was inherently inquisitive. He wanted to learn about the company, the potential for additional training, and opportunities to grow personally and professionally. He was someone who would never be satisfied with the bare minimum, because he was always striving to learn more or something different and wasn't afraid to ask why—even during an interview with the owner of the company. The other traits that I admired in Jacob were the combination of a strong sense of self and confidence with just enough humility. He understood that as a 22-year-old he still had a lot to learn. I hired him on the spot."

Some additional tips:

- If it's not too personal and you find something in common with your interviewer, mention it. For example, if you see a photo of him in Disney World and you just got back from a trip there, you might make a comment or ask a question. Or perhaps your interviewer shares a passion for your favorite sports team. Try to make a connection.[iii]

- Don't reveal too many personal details about yourself unless asked. This is supposed to be about your experience and competence. Do not bring up anything about politics or religion.

- Don't be embarrassed to ask the interviewer to clarify a question you don't understand or to pause before you answer. It's better to take a few seconds to prepare your response than to answer too quickly.

- It's okay to take occasional notes on specific points you want to follow up on or ask about.

[iii] Writer, Staff. "Women—12 Tips to Ace Your Job Interview." *Educate to Advance.* 3 June 2017 Web. http://www.educatetoadvance.com/women-12-tips-to-ace-your-job-interview/

- If something important to your candidacy wasn't asked, find a way to bring it up.
- Always send a thank-you note. More on that to follow.

6.7: What to Do After the Interview?

Following an interview, you must always send a thank-you note, even if you feel it won't be read or the interviewer won't care. It's understood that admissions counselors at the most popular universities interview hundreds of students and are busy, but oftentimes thank-you notes do get to them, and many make a positive note of it! The note can be short and sweet or more detailed if you feel you made a good connection with the interviewer. Even if you feel the interview didn't go well, you should still send the interviewer a thank-you note. There are differing opinions as to whether the note should be sent via email or via a handwritten note on stationery through the regular mail. This can be a judgment call. If the interviewer is on the younger side and you think an email is fine, then send an email. If you had the sense the interviewer was a bit more old-fashioned, then a handwritten note might just be the way to go. Also, if this was for an interview at a large university that receives thousands upon thousands of applications each year, an email might be best because it can take weeks for the general mail to be sorted, and therefore it could take weeks for the interviewer to receive your note.

YOUR TURN 6.2

Preparing A Thank-You Note

Directions: It is always wise to follow up an interview by sending a thank-you note to the person(s) who interviewed you. Try to do so as soon as possible so that the interviewer will remember who you were. If you made a real connection and there was a lot of conversation, you can feel free to add details and make the note longer in nature. If the interview was on the shorter side or you didn't have a lot of small talk to connect on, that is okay too. You should still send a brief note, as it shows respect.

Example Note to College Admissions Interviewer

Dear Mr./Ms./Mrs./Dr./Dean "Last Name":

Thank you so much for the time you provided to me during my recent interview. I especially enjoyed learning (insert some detail here) about your university. I also found (some other fact) interesting (or exciting). I feel that I am a good fit for your school because (insert some reason). I hope to have the opportunity to attend (insert name of school).

Sincerely,
(your full name, name of the high school you attend)

Example Note to Job Interviewer

Dear Mr./Ms./Mrs./Dr. "Last Name" (or if you feel it was clear you should address them by first name then you can do so):

I wanted to take a moment to thank you for the time you provided to me during my interview. I especially enjoyed learning (insert some detail here) about the company. I also found (some other fact) interesting (or exciting). I feel that I am a good fit for your (company/organization) because (insert some reason).

Sincerely,
(your full name)

6.8: The Take Away

- Going for an interview is a big deal and includes more than just being able to answer questions. Be well rested, appropriately dressed, on time, and prepared by having practiced with some other trusted individual!

- Know what kinds of questions to anticipate and have some answers ready.

- Be prepared to also ask questions of the interviewer.

- Remember to use your social skills. Make eye contact, shake hands, and say please and thank you.

- Be sure to follow up any interview with a thank-you note!

BUILDING A SOLID EMOTIONAL INTELLIGENCE/EQ

7.1: IQ, EQ, and Personality Make Who You Are

Your IQ, or intelligence quotient, is your ability to learn and typically doesn't change much over the course of your lifetime. Your EQ, or emotional intelligence, is a flexible set of skills that can be acquired and improved with practice. While you can develop a high emotional intelligence even if you aren't born with it, you can't predict emotional intelligence based on how smart someone is. Personality is the final piece that makes you who you are. Personality is the result of hardwired preferences. Personality usually doesn't change much over your lifetime. According to Drs. Travis Bradberry and Jean Greaves, authors of *Emotional Intelligence 2.0*, "Emotional intelligence is your ability to recognize and understand emotions in yourself and others and your ability to use this awareness to manage your behavior and relationships." Your emotional intelligence is the foundation for a host of critical skills—it impacts most everything you say and do each day.[i]

[i] Writer, Staff. "About Emotional Intelligence." *TalentSmart.* 8 May 2017. Web. http://www.talentsmart.com/about/emotional-intelligence.php

7.2: Don't Employers Want Smart Employees?

Of course they do! However, more and more employers are looking for employees who are smart and competent in their professional skills AND highly competent in "soft skills" or skills that can be best described by an emotional quotient. Soft skills are a group of personality traits that character-ize one's ability to interact with other people. These skills can include social graces, communication abilities, language skills, personal habits, cognitive or emotional empathy, and leadership traits.

They are qualities and skills that cannot be measured on any standard-ized test and yet are highly valued by academic institutions and businesses. Some of them may sound familiar because they are the very same skills you learned in kindergarten and were evaluated on in school or for your college admission. They are the same skills that we talked about in Chapter 2. They have been important character traits for every generation, and they will con-tinue to rank right up there as important skills to possess because you will need them for future success. Many employers try to maximize their hiring practices by hiring people who already have these skills. In fact, a company called TalentSmart tested more than a million people and found that the upper echelons of top performance are filled with people who are high in emotional intelligence—90 percent of top performers, to be exact. They also discovered that EQ is responsible for 58 percent of your job performance, and those employees with high EQ tend to earn $29,000 a year more than their lower EQ counterparts.[ii]

7.3: What Skills Will Increase My EQ?

According to a new CareerBuilder survey, the top 10 skills companies say they look for when hiring a candidate include someone who has a strong work ethic, is dependable, has a positive attitude, is self-motivated, is team-oriented, is organized/can manage multiple priorities, works well under pressure, is an effective communicator, is flexible, and is confident.[iii] Other important skills and character traits include compassion, kindness, re-sponsibility, empathy, good manners, respect, gratitude, inquisitiveness, love of learning, courage, common sense, spirituality, diligence, grit, resilience,

---

[ii] Schmidt, Mike. "Emotional Intelligence (EQ) Stats." Web. 2017. www.emotionalintelligence.net

[iii] Grasz, J. "Overwhelming Majority of Companies Say Soft Skills Are Just as Important as Hard Skills, According to a New CareerBuilder Survey." *CareerBuilder*. 10 April 2014. Web. 10 May 2017. http://www .careerbuilder.com/share/aboutus/pressreleasesdetail.aspx?ed=12/31/2014&id=pr817&sd=4/10/2014

persistence, creativity, life skills, discernment, integrity, patience, self-control, leadership, and a sense of humor.

Whether you know it or not, you have been practicing and building your EQ skills in your family life, in school, on the playground, on sports teams, and any time you interact with other people. Face it … there are some people who naturally get along with everyone. You know who these people are. They tend to have very strong interpersonal skills and can pretty much float in and out of different groups of people with little or no effort. Other people have to work harder to develop social skills and relationships with a variety of personalities. The good news is that even if "interpersonal skills" are not your natural strength, they can be enhanced and developed with some effort and practice. Developing these skills can lead to a higher EQ, which will serve you well in future relationships.

7.4: Reading Body Language

Travis Bradberry, president of TalentSmart, wrote a piece for *Entrepreneur* where he shares that reading body language is a critical skill, and that those who are able to read body language can have an edge or advantage in the workplace: [iv]

Bradberry goes on to highlight the following important research, "According to UCLA research, only 7 percent of communication is based on the actual words we say. As for the rest, 38 percent comes from tone of voice and the remaining 55 percent comes from body language. If you can become aware of and accurately interpret that 55 percent, you will be a step ahead."[v]

Before you lose sleep over the idea of having to be a body language expert, realize that you have probably in some way or another been reading body language most of your life. Think of a time when you did something your parents were very unhappy with. They may have raised their voice, or maybe they were even yelling at you. Along with that, you probably also noticed that their face was turning red or they were waving their arms around. Now think of a time when they were disappointed with you. They probably told you they were disappointed, but then maybe they turned away from you or wouldn't make eye contact. Now think of a time when they were very happy with something you did. Maybe they hugged you, or their eyes crinkled in the corner because they had such a huge smile.

[iv] Bradberry, T. "8 Great Tricks for Reading People's Body Language." *Entrepreneur.* 18 May 2016. Web. 8 May 2017. https://www.entrepreneur.com/article/275309

[v] Bradberry, T. "8 Great Tricks for Reading People's Body Language." *Entrepreneur.* 18 May 2016. Web. 8 May 2017. https://www.entrepreneur.com/article/275309

Here are some common body language cues:
External or Physical Signs That May Signal Anger/Frustration:

- Crossed or waving arms
- Tight or clenched fists
- Crossed legs
- Red face
- Facial or jaw muscles visibly twitching
- Eyebrows furrowed
- Leaning in toward you or getting "in your face"

External Signs That May Signal Disagreement or Annoyance:

- Turning away from you
- Not making eye contact
- Rolling eyes
- Shaking their head side to side
- Starting to do something else while you are still talking
- Slumping down in a chair or in posture if standing

External Signs That May Signal Happiness or Approval:

- A smile
- Good eye contact
- An upright and engaged posture
- Nodding their head up and down in agreement
- Reaching in for a handshake

In order to be able to read body language well, the first step is to be aware that people can and do give signals about their feelings via external signs. Once you are aware, you can begin watching the people with whom you interact more closely. One thing is for sure, if you notice a shift in physical demeanor or tone of voice, chances are something is going on! It might even be a good idea to state that you feel like something is wrong, but you are not sure what. This then opens the door to communicating more clearly.

Mary's Story...

Mary (to her roommate): Ugh, I am so annoyed. We have a group project that we are working on in microeconomics, and today during our group meeting, we were each reporting in on what we have gotten done. Andrea, the person we designated as the group leader, was sitting in her chair, all slumped down with her arms crossed, and I could see her jaw muscle twitching.

JoAnn (roommate): Wow, what do you think that was about?

Mary: Well, I know I only got done about half of what I said I would during last week's meeting, and one of the other group members hadn't actually done anything at all on his list.

JoAnn: Oh, well I am guessing she cares about her grade and feels annoyed. She probably feels like people aren't pulling their weight.

Mary: Well, then why didn't she just say that?

JoAnn: Some people are not comfortable confronting others when they are unhappy. I think you should talk to Mary and the other group members and agree that things have slipped from the plan a bit and develop a new plan to get back on track.

7.5: Developing Personal and Social Competence

Personal competence is your ability to focus on your self-awareness and self-management skills more than on your interactions with other people. This means being aware of your emotions, body language, and tendencies and then managing your behaviors appropriately to stay flexible and positive. Social competence is your ability to understand other people's moods, behavior, and motives in order to improve the quality of your relationships. Can you pick up on emotions in other people and understand what is really going on? Can you read their body language and use it to assess how the conversation is progressing? Can you manage relationships with others by being aware of their feelings and navigating the relationship to a positive outcome?[vi]

[vi] Writer, Staff. "About Emotional Intelligence." *TalentSmart.* 8 May 2017. Web. http://www.talentsmart.com/about/emotional-intelligence.php

7.6: Understanding and Managing Emotions

All of us react to situations with a variety of emotions. However, there are only a few basic emotions: anger, sorrow, joy, surprise, fear, disgust, guilt/shame, and interest. All of the others are learned and are usually some combination of the basic emotions.[vii] We feel our emotions as we react to something that we hear, see, and/or experience. Our perception of that event strikes a chord in us, and we usually feel something—positive or negative. Once in a while, we may feel ambivalent. Sometimes our emotional reaction is very clear to those around us. For example, a parent who is watching her daughter score the winning goal in a hockey game will probably react with loud cheering and jumping up and down. It would be easy to conclude that she is proud of and happy for her daughter. However, have you ever seen somebody who is not happy with an airline attendant? Lost luggage or a missed flight can cause a variety of emotions—none of which is probably positive! Managing emotions, despite annoying, frustrating, and aggravating situations, is an art. Some people do it very well, but they have practiced for a long time to master the skill of calm and rational behavior. This is because they understand the importance of being mindful of what is happening around them and making sure that they are in the right mindset for a positive situation/outcome.

7.7: What Are Mindsets?

There are three primary states of mind: Emotional Mind, Rational Mind, and Wise Mind.[viii] Understanding these three mindsets is critical when communicating with others. Emotional intelligence is a balance between Emotional and Rational Mind and is called Wise Mind.

Emotional Mind

When a person is in Emotional Mind, emotions are controlling behavior and thinking. Facts may be distorted and logical thinking may be difficult. Sometimes the energy of the behavior may match the intensity of the feelings. On the positive side, emotions help us feel connected with others. Emotions are at the root of relationships and allow us to feel empathy for

[vii] Dietz, L. "Myths About Emotions." Web. 08 May 2017. https://dbtselfhelp.com/html/myths.html
[viii] Dietz, L. "Mind States." Web. 08 May 2017. https://www.dbtselfhelp.com/html/mind_states.html

others. However, sometimes when we are in Emotional Mind, we don't always see clearly and may have "black and white" or "all or nothing" thinking. This can lead to short-term gains but long-term consequences, including regrets for things said or done in anger. Factors that can negatively affect Emotional Mind are illness, hunger, lack of sleep, being overscheduled or overwhelmed with tasks, or substance abuse.[ix]

Rational Mind

When a person is using Rational Mind, she is approaching things intellectually and is thinking logically. There is focused attention and a bit of detachment when in Rational Mind so that one can get the job done. There is no emotion when solving a problem due to a "just the facts" mentality. When in Rational Mind, much can be accomplished. However, there is a downside to being in Rational Mind too often/too much.[x] Hollywood helps us understand an overacting Rational Mind with the character of Sheldon on *The Big Bang Theory*. If you know that show, you will recognize that Sheldon approaches everything with analysis and logic. Everything! Unfortunately, he is perceived by some as being rigid, cold, and boring. He does not appear to have empathy and often alienates others with his statements of the facts without regard for how they might be perceived by others.

Wise Mind

When one achieves Wise Mind, there is a sense of peace within. Wise Mind is a blend of Emotional Mind and Rational Mind and is truly the place you want to be whenever possible. Everyone has Wise Mind, but some of you may not have found it yet or use it often. Wise Mind is an intuition, a feeling of knowing what's right—in your gut, in your heart, or in your mind. It's important to find this sense of calmness that comes with feeling good about a decision or path forward. You can let go of intense emotions so that you have a sense of wisdom inside you.[xi]

[ix] Dietz, L. "Mind States." Web. 08 May 2017. https://www.dbtselfhelp.com/html/mind_states.html
[x] Dietz, L. "Mind States." Web. 08 May 2017. https://www.dbtselfhelp.com/html/mind_states.html
[xi] Dietz, L. "Mind States." Web. 08 May 2017. https://www.dbtselfhelp.com/html/mind_states.html

VOICES FROM CAMPUS 7.2

Bill Is Upset…

John (to roommate): Wow, did you see Bill huffing and puffing around the kitchen this morning slamming drawers and the dishwasher, seriously, what was that all about?

Mark (roommate): Yeah, that was kind of ridiculous, especially when he was like, "Wow, I hope I can find some dishes to cook dinner with later."

John: Ohhhh. I was supposed to load and run the dishwasher last night and I didn't, and actually I forgot the last time I was supposed to as well.

Mark: Oh, well I guess he's pretty ticked then.

John: Yeah, I guess so. I don't know what the big deal is. He can always just get some dinner in the cafeteria tonight.

Mark: Oh, he doesn't have a partial meal plan. Like, his parents won't pay for it—they said he either needs to eat on campus or do his own cooking at the apartment. And he also told me yesterday that he has three tests today.

John: Oh, I didn't realize that he didn't have a partial meal plan or that he has three tests today, so I guess it is a big deal to him that there are no clean dishes to cook with. I guess I owe him an apology. Hopefully, he'll get over it. Maybe I'll buy takeout tonight to try to make it up to him.

YOUR TURN 7.1

Be A Body Language Detective

Directions: Using the chart below, consider the following scenario and see if you can identify the purpose of the behavior and how you could best handle the situation.[xii]

Example

You share an apartment with three other guys. Dave is a newcomer to the group and is driving everyone nuts. He is always questioning the grocery bill, wanting to see every little receipt, and demanding that certain brand-name items

[xii] Writer, Staff. "The 4 Goals of Misbehavior in Children." *Metta Psychology Group.* 18 January 2017. Web. 29 May 2017. http://www.mettapsych.com/news/2017/1/18/the-4-goals-of-misbehavior-in-children

be purchased rather than the store-brand items. He has even questioned Mike, who has served as the "keeper of the checkbook" for the past two years with no problem. Now, Dave wants to see the checkbook every month. And to top it off, just yesterday, when the guys were discussing the purchase of a new couch from the local thrift shop for next semester, he went off on a tirade about spending too much money and insisted that he do comparison shopping at a variety of stores. How do you feel in this situation? Are you annoyed, angry, or hurt?

Why is Dave acting this way? Is he trying to gain your attention, get power and control, or get even with you?

How should the roommates handle this ongoing situation so that it is a win–win for everyone? Based on your answers above, use the chart to help you respond in a "wise minded" manner.

Now think about a challenging/frustrating scenario you were recently in. Using the chart below, see if you can figure out what was really at the heart of the behavior and how you could respond.

If you feel ...	The person is ...	Your response ...
beyond irritated and annoyed	trying to get your attention and wants to be recognized	When possible, offer recognition and positive reinforcement for the smallest accomplishment to build the person's self-confidence. On the flip side, inappropriate, attention-seeking behaviors will need to be ignored or dealt with in a tactful, but firm manner.
angry and threatened and find yourself starting to be defensive	trying to gain control or power over the situation or you	Sometimes when people feel the need to always be in control, they really are anxious and insecure on the inside. Controlling the outside environment is their way (maybe without even knowing it) of making life predictable. Then they don't have to deal with the unknown or what is to come. Giving them choices or asking their opinion may be helpful in letting them have some control within necessary parameters. These people tend not to do well "off the cuff," when something is sprung on them without warning, or in new or unfamiliar situations.
hurt, disappointed, shocked, or appalled	trying to get even or seek revenge	These people may be hurting inside. Use reflective listening skills and acknowledge any misunderstandings and hurt feelings. Build trust. Show that you care. Recognize and encourage strengths.

7.8: How Do I Develop a Wise Mind and Higher EQ?

Observe your own thoughts and emotions. Be aware of every thought, feeling, or action that comes through your mind. Be in the present—what is happening right now—rather than worrying about the past or future.

Describe your feelings or thoughts. I am feeling sad. I am filled with sadness. Then describe what happened. Was it a thought? An action? A feeling? Call it what it is. NOTE: You can observe and describe your thoughts without taking action.When observing and describing your thoughts, remember to focus on just the facts. Leave out opinions and do not be judgmental of yourself or others.

Practice your skills until they become a part of who you are. You want to be able to avoid potentially explosive situations by changing your reaction or response. Practicing is easier when you are doing one thing at a time. For example, if you are reading, read. If you are eating, eat. If you are with a group of friends, be with the group. When you multitask, it divides your attention making it difficult to do justice to either task.

Let go of … distractions, getting even, or useless anger and revenge. Instead, focus on what works and try to end up with a "win–win" situation rather than someone being "right" or "wrong." And that word *fair*? Back in kindergarten you might have learned that "Fair isn't equal. Fair is giving each person what she needs." At least, that is the hope. But even then, sometimes life just isn't fair. If you are in Wise Mind, you will try to act skillfully in your current situation, not the situation you wish you were in. But it takes practice. Lots of practice. Consider that when learning something new, it takes at least 30 repetitions of the same skill, usually practiced in the same way each day. So don't be too hard on yourself if it is taking time to find your Wise Mind. As long as you are using it sometimes, you are on the right path. Having a Wise Mind will not only increase your EQ but also put you on the road to success.[xiii]

7.9: When All Else Fails, Drop the Rope

There is a great story called *Tug-of-War With a Monster*.[xiv] The monster is big, ugly, and very strong. In between you and the monster is a pit, and as far as you can tell, it is bottomless. If you lose this tug-of-war, you will fall into the pit and be destroyed. So you pull and pull, but the harder you pull, the

[xiii] Dietz, L. "Mind States." Web. 08 May 2017. https://www.dbtselfhelp.com/html/mind_states.html
[xiv] Hayes, S. C., Strosahl, K., & Wilson, K. G. *Acceptance and Commitment Therapy: An Experiential Approach to Behavior Change*. New York: Guilford Press, 1999, p. 109.

harder the monster pulls, and you edge closer and closer to the pit. Who is going to fall into the pit? Hopefully, no one, but sometimes the hardest thing to see is that our job here is not to win the tug-of-war … our job is to drop the rope. You can't drop the rope when you are in the Emotional Mind state. Maybe you can when you are in the Rational Mind state, or maybe you can't. But when you are in the Wise Mind state, you are calm. You know somewhere inside that this tug-of-war, this battle, isn't worth falling into the pit. You know that you have to detach and look at the situation with your mind's eye and use the wisdom from within.[xv]

Figure 7.1 Graphic of Tug of War With a Monster

7.10: Using Your Wise Mind to Get Along With Your Roommate

Having a roommate is something that most college students will ex- perience. If you come from a big family or have shared a bedroom or bathroom with a sibling, it might be an easier transition. Many schools have surveys and ways to match up prospective roommates based on preferences. You might even be able to room with someone you know, even if she isn't a best friend. However, even in the best of situations, there can be problems. Here are some "Wise Mind" tips that might help you

[xv] Writer, Staff. "Tug of War with the Anxiety Monster." *The Career Psychologist.* 3 June 2012. Web. 9 May 2017. http://www.thecareerpsychologist.com/tug-of-war-with-the-anxiety-monster/

avoid potential problems and develop a positive roommate situation. Some of them you learned in … yes, in kindergarten!

- Be clear about expectations—yours and your roommate's. If you are a neat freak, say so. If you have to have it pitch dark and silent to sleep, say so. It's better to put these things out on the table at the start than to stew on them until you explode. That would be Emotional Mind and we don't want that, right?

- Remember the Golden Rule. Treat others as you wish to be treated!

- Be respectful of your roommate and your roommate's things. This includes being mindful of who you bring into your room and how often.

- Be responsible. Lock doors and windows. You would feel awful if your negligence caused your roommate's possessions (or yours) to be stolen.

- Be open to new ideas and things. Don't be judgmental. You may be amazed at the experiences you can have because of a roommate from another culture or with different interests.

- Be friendly, but don't expect your roommate to be your best friend. Some of the best roommate situations are with individuals who aren't best friends but just friendly and respectful of each other.

- Address problems when they are little before they become big. If you stuff them inside and don't talk about them, Emotional Mind will likely emerge, and it won't be a pretty sight! [xvi]

[xvi] Writer, Staff. "How Not to Kill Your College Roommate." *Unigo.* 2 June 2015. Web. 9 May 2017. https://www.unigo.com/in-college/campus-life/how-not-to-kill-your-college-roommate

VOICES FROM CAMPUS 7.3

Roommate Turned Best Friend…

Freshman: When I found out who my roommate was, we started to communicate by email and eventually spoke on the phone. He was from India, so it was hard for me to understand him and doubly hard to talk on the phone due to the time difference. I was a little nervous about sharing a room with a stranger as I never had done that before. I got there before he did and selected my bed, dresser, and closet and unpacked. He arrived the next day. He flew to the United States by himself and didn't have anyone to help with his things. But then he only had two suitcases. My mom had packed enough supplies and food for an army, so I was happy to share. He was very quiet, but I am probably loud enough for both of us. In the beginning, it was hard to communicate. He seemed a little sad. But in time, he seemed to be more comfortable. By Thanksgiving, we had come to find a peaceful coexistence, and I learned that he was actually older than I was and had already earned a degree in India. He was definitely smarter than I was in science, so he was a big help with my chemistry course. I invited him to come home with me for Thanksgiving dinner, which he did. My mom loved him! He visited relatives in another state for Christmas. The following summer, he invited me to visit his family in India. It was a fabulous experience, and I never would have had the chance to visit India without having Sim as a roommate. We are still really good friends. Sim and my mom still keep in touch on Facebook!

Oftentimes, roommates rent an apartment and then there are more responsibilities to share. All of the previous suggestions still hold true, but consider these tips for peaceful living without any one roommate bearing the brunt of financial obligations or consequences.[xvii]

- Discuss and post house rules. This is not only important to be respectful of everyone living in the house but to cover yourself legally and financially. You are responsible for your apartment. Damages will come out of your deposit and you will be charged for anything over

[xvii] Pullman, E. "Secrets of Successful Roommate Relationships." *The Huffington Post.* 18 November 2013. Web. 9 May 2017. http://www.huffingtonpost.com/elizabeth-pietrzak/secrets-of-successful-roo_b_4278163.html

and above that amount. You want to make sure no one will cause you to lose your housing or jeopardize your financial investment.

- Discuss deal breakers up front. If you are opposed to smoking in the apartment, say so in the beginning. Also, be respectful of everyone's work and class schedules. For example, just because you have off on Wednesdays, don't have a party Tuesday night. Your roommates may have an early class on Wednesday morning.

- When renting an apartment with others, you will need furniture and kitchen things. Decide how you want to stock and furnish the apartment. If you aren't going to sell everything when you break up housekeeping, it might be better to bring your own bedroom items and any other big-ticket items someone might have. For example, if Steve has a couch, then he brings it and takes it when the lease expires. Same thing would hold true with kitchen items. What you bring, you take or get rid of. If the group has to purchase something, like a rug, then you can decide as a group what to do with it when you vacate the apartment.

- Post a weekly chore chart and share responsibilities.

- Post a log of apartment expenses (or share in an online folder) so that everyone is aware of money going out and money coming in. It usually works out best if one person acts as the treasurer/payer of bills/keeper of money.

- If one tenant is notoriously late with rent checks, electric bill, etc., then consider setting up a payment system such as SQUARE Cash, Venmo, or PayPal so that person's share of the expenses don't fall on the others.

- Food can be the source of issues. Decide how you want to handle this. You can all contribute to the "food fund" each week and do an apartment shopping trip—everyone gets what they want out of that money but the food is fair game for all. Or you can all do your own shopping and have your own shelf in the refrigerator or in the pantry. Or maybe it's a combination of both. However, just remember to be open and honest. If your favorite Ben and Jerry's ice cream is off-limits, you had better make that clear from the get-go!

7.11: What If I Get a Roommate, Professor, or Boss From You Know Where

Sometimes students encounter a roommate, classmate, course, or professor that proves challenging. It's important that you not let any confusion or misunderstandings go on for too long or your relationship or grade may suffer. This is the time to speak to your professor face to face. Stop in during office hours or make an appointment. Communication is always easier and more productive during face-to-face meetings. If you are sincere in your attempt to improve your understanding of the material or the professor's teaching style/expectations, it will be obvious to your teacher that you are trying. This might allow her to view you as someone who is taking the initiative, leading to more empathy for your situation. This is not the time to rely on emails for communication. If appropriate, regular attendance and participation in class will also demonstrate your work ethic and perseverance. Remember, sometimes the way you handle an obstacle or challenge will be a feather in your cap in the future. This professor just might be your best letter of recommendation because of your diligence, hard work, and willingness to be a team player in your own education. She might see you as someone who doesn't give up and goes out of your way to seek out resources and be a problem solver ... all good EQ qualities to have.

Chances are you will encounter difficult people in your life, whether they are roommates, a professor, colleagues at work, or neighbors. That's life. But our hope is that by using your Wise Mind and a few simple suggestions, you will be able to navigate these challenges and not let the negativity drag you down.

Remember these important tips:

- You do not want to unleash the Emotional Mind, so remain calm and cool and drop the rope. Don't engage. Take a deep breath. Count to 10. Walk away for a bit.

- You might have heard the expression, "You can't fly like an eagle if you hang out with turkeys." Surround yourself with positive people and avoid the "turkeys." Pick your battles. Some battles aren't worth fighting.

- Detach and don't personalize. Remember, spray on the Teflon and let annoying behaviors and words slide right off of you.

- Try to be proactive rather than reactive. You can do this by widening your perspective of a situation, which will reduce the possibility of a misperception. For example, if a colleague never responds to an email in a timely matter, you could think, "Wow, she must be really annoyed with my question or me." Or you could think, "Wow, she must be so busy this time of the year. I bet she will respond as soon as she can." You never know what others may be facing … an illness, a crisis at home, who knows. But sometimes giving someone the benefit of the doubt can help alleviate frustration and blame. If you have to address the situation, use an "I message" such as, "I felt confused when I didn't get a response to my email. I'm not sure if you got it, need more time to respond, have just been busy, or are annoyed for some reason. Can you please help me understand?"

- Eleanor Roosevelt said, "No one can make you feel inferior without your consent." So when you are dealing with aggressive, bullying types, consider that their behavior is their problem, not yours. Chances are, they are trying to put you down or find fault with your work to make themselves look better. They are usually looking to gain power or control. If you react by being on the defense and allow the Emotional Mind to take over, you will just give them more power. Sometimes deflecting and shifting the spotlight onto them will help. You can ask probing questions or, when appropriate, compliment something that they did. You can also use the Rational Mind and separate the person from the situation. Using logical thinking and looking at the facts, you will know that nothing will come of a discussion where there is anger or yelling. Try suggesting that the meeting end for now and reconvene later when everyone is calm.[xviii]

  However, if the bullying or aggressive behavior continues, it needs to be addressed. Be sure to place yourself in a position where you can safely stand up for yourself. In cases of physical, verbal, or emotional abuse, consult with a school/university counselor, law enforcement, administrative professionals, or legal personnel. It's

[xviii] Ni, P. "Ten Keys to Handling Unreasonable & Difficult People." *Psychology Today*. 2 September 2013. Web. 9 May 2017. https://www.psychologytoday.com/blog/communication-success/201309/ten-keys-handling-unreasonable-difficult-people

very important to stand up to bullies, and you don't have to do it alone.

• Above all, maintain a sense of humor when dealing with unfriendly or difficult people. Humor can break the ice in many awkward situations, and when there are smiles and laughter, people usually lighten up and feel better.

YOUR TURN 7.2

Creating Win-Win Situations

Directions: Keep a "mindset log" for a week. Note situations that arise and your reactions to them.

Note when you are in different mindsets and how you reacted. Consider if your reactions were the best way to elicit a "win–win" scenario for all who were involved or if you could have done something different. When you find yourself in "Wise Mind," give yourself a pat on the back, because it's not an easy place to live and will take practice and time. Any path toward that mindset is worthy of celebration.

Mindset Log

Date	Place Situation Occurred	People Involved	What happened?	Mindset Used (circle)	Next time I will try to ...	Comments Suggestions Celebrations
				Emotional Rational Wise		
				Emotional Rational Wise		
				Emotional Rational Wise		
				Emotional Rational Wise		

7.12: The Take Away

- Your EQ, or emotional intelligence, is as important as how smart you are, if not more so.

- Employers prefer to hire employees who already have high EQ skills.

- EQ skills can be developed by

  - understanding and using body language to your advantage,

  - developing your personal and social competencies, and

  - understanding and managing your emotions.

- A higher EQ will help you be successful in future relationships and professional endeavors and could actually increase your earning potential.

Image Credit

FINALLY ...
NETWORKING, JOB
HUNTING, AND
THE REAL WORLD

inally! After all these years and hard work, the time has come to apply for a job. A real job. A job that will allow you to become a successful, independent adult. You are ready to join the real world and go to work instead of class. Although, if you can find something that brings you joy, something that you are passionate about, you will never really feel like you've worked a day in your life. Figure out what tasks you enjoy and what you're good at doing. Then try to find a job that plays to your strengths. Don't focus on the job title or industry. Look at what the job DOES on a daily basis. You'll ultimately be more successful when you do something you're good at and enjoy.

You have worked hard and are about to receive a diploma and/or a post-graduate degree(s). You have taken all the required courses and completed the practicums, internships, or student teaching, and now you are about to graduate. You are ready . . . or are you? This is a time when even the most prepared student might have just a bit of trepidation.

When putting together a résumé, networking with other professionals, job hunting, and actually applying for a job, there are many well-documented words of wisdom from people in the know. CEO's of large tech companies, hiring managers, those at LinkedIn, professors at colleges, owners of businesses, and administrators in the field of education all seem to offer similar advice. This chapter offers a broad overview of that advice.

8.1: A Résumé That Stands Out

In Chapter 5, you were provided with information as to how to build a résumé, but now you need to create one that is going to stand out from the pack. As you have likely heard, your will be just one of many to be screened either via online submission or by hand. It is critical to submit all the required documents in full, and usually along with a cover letter that isn't just a repeat of the résumé. It must relate your skills and interests to the job that is posted. It should reflect your accomplishments in other relevant experiences and, above all else, it must be error free. This includes any email communications, too. One spelling or mechanical error or any unprofessional communications could land your résumé and/or cover letter in the rejections pile. Make sure that you have also correctly spelled the name of the person to whom it's addressed, and do not be too informal. For example, when contacting a potential employer, do not make the mistake of addressing him by first name. No matter how young he may look or be, your initial greeting needs to be by the surname (Mr., Mrs., Miss, Ms., Dr. etc.). If the person is comfortable being addressed by first name, he will tell you. It's not a liberty you can just assume to take.

VOICES FROM CAMPUS 8.1

A Simple Mistake Can Be Big…

Shane: So have you heard anything about the job you applied to?

Mark: Oh man, I did and something really embarrassing happened. Remember I told you my neighbor told me about the job and how the hiring manager was a friend of his?

Shane: Oh, right.

Mark: Well, I sent off my résumé with a cover letter directly to the guy. Since my neighbor had told me his first and last name, I addressed it to him by his first name. So my neighbor tells me the next day he heard from his friend and that he thought my résumé was "okay" but that it was rubbing him a bit the wrong way that I just called him by his first name. He said he wants to wait and see what other résumés come in, and maybe I will hear from him. I didn't really think through that I should have addressed him formally. It isn't like he was my friend. I hope I still have a shot!

Your résumé is never really finished. It is always a "work in progress." Do not think you can have one résumé and apply to 100 different jobs. In fact, *US News* contributor and founder of Jobhuntercoach, Arnie Fertig, references John Sullivan, a thought leader in the human resources field: "'As a result of not actually spending the necessary time reviewing and side-by-side comparing the requirements to their own qualifications, job applicants end up applying for many jobs where they have no chance of being selected.' When you apply to anything and everything, it shouldn't come as a surprise when you wind up with nothing!" [i, ii]

Most big companies with recruiting departments review every résumé they receive. However, they usually spend less than a minute on each résumé. The ones that generally get passed to hiring managers are those that clearly fit the requirements of the job posting. Remember, recruiters don't necessarily have the time or technical knowledge to "make the leap" that you might assume seems obvious. They are reviewing tons of résumés, so be sure to make any and all connections for them. They look for keywords and matches between the skills that the hiring manager needs and what the candidate has on the résumé. As mentioned in Chapter 5, you must customize your résumé for each position for which you are applying. The résumé

[i] Sullivan, J. "Why You Can't Get A Job … Recruiting Explained by the Numbers." *ERE Media.* 20 May 2013. Web. 21 May 2017. https://www.ere.net/why-you-cant-get-a-job-recruiting-explained-by-the-numbers/
[ii] Fertig, A. "The 10 Best Websites to Find Jobs." U.S. News & World Report. 27 October 2015. Web. http://money.usnews.com/money/blogs/outside-voices-careers/2015/10/27/the-10-best-websites-to-find-jobs

needs to accentuate items and traits that are listed in the specific job description. It should be well formatted, visually appealing, and easy to read. Consider using LinkedIn to look at current employees in the same or similar role or department to which you're applying and customize your résumé based on what you discover about people currently in that job. Always have someone with experience in the field review your résumé to make sure the keywords that résumé filters look for are highlighted.

If your résumé is passed on to those who do the hiring, they tend to look at previous experiences to see if there is a fit to the current vacancy. For example, an employer might evaluate the résumé as a whole and check to make sure your work reflects the qualities needed in the role for which you're applying. If the job requires attention to detail, then the employer might immediately cut résumés with typos, inconsistent formatting, or an extra blank page.

8.2: How Should I Start Looking for a Job?

Having a résumé is only half the battle. One of the great advantages of the Internet is that searching for a job is easier than ever before. Try using major websites that list thousands of jobs, such as Monster.com, Careerbuilder.com, LinkedIn, or Indeed.com. If you are focused on a certain field such as a career in biotech or pharmaceuticals, look for websites that list jobs specifically in that industry (e.g., medzilla.com). If you know which companies you want to work for, then of course you can search directly for jobs posted on their website. And if all else fails and you are really struggling to find a job, consider working with a recruiting agency as these tend to be more local or regional in nature. Do a general search for local career recruiting agencies in your area.[iii]

8.3: Top Tips From Employers

Tip #1—Search early and often. Many companies start recruiting employees in senior year, but some even look at sophomores and juniors. This is especially true for paid and unpaid internships.

iii Fertig, A. "The 10 Best Websites to Find Jobs." U.S. News & World Report. 27 October 2015. Web. http://money.usnews.com/money/blogs/outside-voices-careers/2015/10/27/the-10-best-websites-to-find-jobs

Tip #2—If you attend a college or university, use the career placement center early and often and make yourself known. Make a list of the companies that interest you and start to research those companies, as well as whether that company has regular contact with your school's career placement center. If your career placement center has the name of a recruiter from that company, consider reaching out to express your interest in the company. Maybe the recruiter plans to come to campus soon and you could meet up.

Tip #3—Play up your "real world" experiences and street smarts whenever possible. Consider sharing relevant experience from class, volunteering, extracurricular activities, previous jobs, and internships. These experiences may not fit well in the actual résumé but often can be worked into a cover letter. Remember to refer back to the content on cover letters in Chapter 5. Sometimes your greatest life challenge will be the most compelling reason someone would want to hire you.

Tip #4—Update your status. Make sure your social networking profiles and online presence are "employer friendly." You never know the age or perspective of that employer so if you wouldn't say it or show it to your parent or grandparent, then keep it off of social media. Err on the side of being neutral and conservative. Many hiring managers look to see what information an applicant has out there on Facebook or Instagram.

Tip #5—Have an "elevator speech." Think of yourself as a salesperson. What are you selling? Your best self! The résumé is actually your sales pitch. However, your "elevator speech" is three to four sentences that outline why you are the perfect person for the job. This is what you would say to a hiring manager who you met on an elevator and who will only allow you the time it takes to go from the ground floor to the third floor to make your pitch. If it's good, he will say "Okay, send me your résumé." Then what follows in the résumé are details like your work experience and accomplishments that support your elevator speech. When possible, it is wise to craft your elevator speech to match the requirements of the job. Craft it so that it's clear to the hiring manager that you are the type of person they are looking for and can be trained to be a contributing member of the company.

Tip #6—Use LinkedIn and other websites for professional networking and job hunting as early as possible in college and add newly acquired skills as you go.

Tip #7—Be patient and at the same time go all out in your search. Exhaust all potential sources for job opportunities. Do not assume you will get a position by applying to four or five positions. It might take 30–40 positions. That's where the need to be patient comes in.

Tip #8—Do your homework. Research companies that you might want to work for. Find companies whose philosophies and culture are a match to your own set of values. Look at what the company owner values in employees and what kind of work environment the company provides. Is family important or are you expected to be on call 24/7? Does the company value community outreach? Is there opportunity for advanced education or training? Is there a mentorship program?

Tip #9—Network! Network! Network!

YOUR TURN 8.1

Design Your Elevator Speech

Directions: Because you never know when the opportunity will arise, draft a three- or four-sentence, 30-second or less elevator speech that you can use in almost any situation. You could always quickly tweak it on the spot for a specific person/situation. This speech should outline who you are, what your goal is, and why any company would want to hire you. Some employers even suggest putting something similar at the top of your résumé rather than an objective statement. An objective statement simply says, "My objective is to work in finance, blah, blah, blah." However, an elevator speech might look more like, "Self-motivated student and resourceful employee capable of multitasking and prioritizing as evidenced by success in balancing a heavy 20-hour workweek while simultaneously maintaining a 3.8 grade point average as a dual major in accounting and finance. Presented with the Outstanding Academic Achievement Award and winner of Sales Associate Appreciation Award. Highly analytical, excellent social skills, and a commitment to quality work."

Regardless of what you decide to put on your résumé, having an elevator speech on the tip of your tongue will help you to be prepared. Here is a website that gives suggestions and examples and might prove helpful: http://idealist-careers.org/a-quick-guide-to-writing-your-elevator-pitch-with-examples/

My Elevator Speech

Who am I?
What is my goal?
Why should you hire me?

Sarah's Story...

Charles, an owner of an engineering company, takes a personal interest in every candidate being considered for employment and always conducts the final technical interview of any possible candidates. He shares this story about Sarah.

"Sarah had an incredible résumé and a 4.0 GPA. She had multiple minors and clearly demonstrated her love of learning and 'type A' personality! However, she explained to me that her parents worked hard to help her go to college so the least she could do was make the most of their money. She always took the maximum number of courses each semester, rather than the minimum, assuring that she would graduate on time. That's how she ended up with several minors. Okay ... she has my attention, and I'm impressed. Again, I put the résumé aside, because I wanted to get to know if Sarah would fit with our company's culture. As soon as I began to ask Sarah a few questions, she began to smile from ear to ear. Sarah had already been on our website and knew our philosophy and culture. For her, our company offered her a dream job because of what we both valued. Sarah did her homework. When she browsed our website, she was delighted to see that family was one of our core fundamentals, and her family was very important to her. It was clear that she would fit right in. She knew it. I knew it. Another outstanding member was added to our professional family."

And from a recent college graduate: "I thought I just gave a company a résumé, talked a little and smiled during the interview—just wing it—and I'd get a great job ... I need to have background information, have questions ready to ask, and be prepared so I'm not taken off guard and also stand out from others."[iv]

8.4: Networking ... Go Ahead and Call Aunt Matilda or Joe From the Gym

You have been building your résumé for several years and now the time has come to use it. Surely, all you have to do is send out or post

[iv] Jacob Levitan, Washington University in St. Louis, Class of 2017 http://www.theroadmap.com/news/Employers-Demand-Soft-Skills.html

that résumé online and you will be contacted for an interview. Right? Wrong! Unless you are very lucky. The absolute best way to get your résumé noticed is through networking—a contact provides an introduction and the résumé is provided as follow-up. In today's job market, where most job openings attract scores of résumés, the chances of landing an interview simply by sending in or posting a résumé are small. If at all possible, a candidate should try to hand deliver the résumé. Sometimes simply showing up can get you noticed. While this may sound a bit old-fashioned especially in the world of electronic submissions, it can still be a viable option for getting noticed, so don't discount delivering your résumé in person.

One of the positive outcomes of technology is the ease with which people can stay in touch with friends and family, as well as establish new connections with "friends of friends" and other people you casually met somewhere. This allows for easy networking and maintaining relationships. Some people are uncomfortable relying on networking or asking for other people's help to land an interview. They feel that it's cheating and that they should be able to get hired on their own merits. This is a needless worry. Looking at these relationships as resources rather than crutches can prove beneficial. You need to pull out all the stops and use whatever resources and contacts you have to allow yourself to stand out. A family friend, that person from your sports team who is now gainfully employed, or a professor or intern supervisor may be just the person to get your résumé pulled from a pile, and at least allow you to receive an invitation to interview. A good word may open a door! From that point on, you are on your own and will have to sell yourself and your skills. Based on your own merits, you will be hired or not, so don't feel that networking somehow makes you less competent. Just remember to express your gratitude to the person who took the time to mentor you or put in a good word for you.

YOUR TURN 8.2

Build Yourself a Board Of Directors

Directions: As a precursor to networking and before you are actually ready to look for a job, consider creating your own Board of Directors. This could happen any time during your school career, sooner if you plan on working right after high school. If you are going to college or a trade school, you might begin early on and then add to or adjust it as you finish your education. These Board Members, or advisors, should be successful people who could be older friends, professors, former managers at summer jobs, alumni, neighbors, etc. Ideally, they would be involved in your particular field of interest, but this is not necessary. Internships and entry-level jobs are wonderful opportunities for getting a "foot in the door." This is a good way to make contacts with established people and develop a reputation as a productive employee. Think about each person you have worked for or collaborated with as a potential member on your Board of Directors. Choose people who you feel have the time and interest to advise and mentor you, and who someday may be willing to connect you to others. Then, remember to touch base and keep them apprised of the progress of your educational successes, internships, and job searches, and listen to any additional advice they might contribute.

Make a list of the names and contact information of those individuals who might be helpful when it's time to network.

Name	Contact Information	Dates Contacted

Networking is part of your life before employment and for the rest of your professional life. *Forbes* magazine offers 10 tips for successful networking:[v]

1. Listen more than you talk.
2. Be curious and ask questions.
3. Get to know the organizers at networking events.
4. Smile!
5. At a networking event, talk to more than one person in the room. There is a natural point when a conversation ends on its own. Recognize it, wrap it up, and move on to meet other people.
6. Focus on how you can help an organization rather than what others can do for you.
7. Try connecting others together, as well as making connections yourself.
8. Be consistent with your networking. Many professions have set meeting times every week/month. Go!
9. Stay patient. Don't force a relationship with someone. They could misinterpret your eagerness as having an ulterior motive.
10. Follow up with other professionals you meet while networking.

8.5: Oh My Gosh, I Have an Interview! Now What?

Chapter 6 is chock full of tips for successful interviewing, so remember to revisit that chapter as often as needed! Employers receive many applications for most open positions. Don't be surprised if you receive a behavioral questionnaire via email before you are actually selected for an interview. These are often used to determine a candidate's fit to the company's culture, work requirements, and values. Also, don't be surprised if your interview is a multi-step process with the initial interview taking place via phone or Skype. Sometimes the process will go beyond two interviews depending on the position, and it might include a team of interviewers. In some situations, like teaching, the candidate may be asked to return and teach a lesson to a class. Most employers are more interested in the candidate's personality,

ᵛ Writer, Staff. "11 Habits the Best Networkers Have." *Forbes.* 24 January 2017. Web. 30 April 2017. https://www.forbes.com/sites/forbescoachescouncil/2017/01/24/11-habits-the-best-networkers-have/#53b9851923a4

inner drive, attitude, teamwork, and leadership abilities than his specific skill level in a particular discipline. Some employers rely heavily on referral candidates, meaning the initial round of interviews is offered to those who have been referred by reliable resources. Most employers do call your reference list, so be sure that you have asked those you have provided as references if they are willing to serve as a positive one for you!

8.6: You're Hired! Tips on Being Successful

When you are so fortunate to be offered a position, focus on the whole company package, not just the paycheck. Consider if there are good opportunities for learning and advancement and other benefits and perks that make the job worthwhile. Is the company a good fit for your values and belief system? A first job may be just a starting place. It may not be the job you dreamed of, but it will give you experience that may lead you to the job you ultimately hope to land. You might find that there are good mentors available who will help you grow and be more marketable in the job you ultimately hope to obtain. As the old adage goes, "it is easier to find a job when you have a job."

Understanding how an office works and getting acclimated to the culture are probably the first big hurdles. Unlike society, where individualism is celebrated, most work settings require a certain level of conformity to the standards, norms, and environment. Some new hires can struggle with picking up on cues and observing how other people interact with them, or they may not readily see how others are viewing them. This is where the need for strong EQ skills kicks in.

However, there is another hurdle that many new graduates are not anticipating and that is being able to self-educate. While many employers build in a certain amount of training for new hires, most employers also expect that new hires will have the ability to do some learning on their own. For example, when asked, many new sales support employees say they are interested in learning more about the customers and the sales process. However, they often interact directly with the sales team and customers on a daily basis and could easily ask questions of the customers or the salespeople themselves.

If, over time, a new employee does not take on more responsibility for learning and performance, he may find that promotions and other opportunities go to others who do. Outside of the business world, many educators report that new teachers seem reluctant to admit that they don't know everything and may need support or further training in specific programs to better meet the needs of their students.

Don't be afraid to ask for help. Most of the time, asking for help is not perceived as a sign of weakness, and most managers or supervisors would much prefer someone ask a question than make a mistake that could have been prevented. If you don't feel like you can go directly to your boss with your questions, see if you can find someone in the company who would be happy to help a new teammate/hire and share his experiences and wisdom. Maybe by joining company-sponsored groups (sports teams, social outings, professional networking, or community service) you can make new friends and also gain unofficial mentors.

Every company has different training methods, and one should take full advantage of them. New employees must clearly understand the organization's standards and what is expected of them. Consider asking for quick and honest performance feedback early on so that you can immediately improve upon or change what isn't meeting expectations. If you don't automatically get feedback, don't be afraid to ask for it.

As has been mentioned in earlier chapters, different age groups tend to perceive and react to situations differently. The following tips may help you avoid miscommunication and discord.

- Never allow idle time at work. Always be working on something. If you don't have anything to work on, ask for more work! Employers notice employees who offer their help for the greater good of the organization.

- Timeliness of responses to any communication. Be aware that a lack of response may be perceived in various ways. The person may be thinking, "I wonder if he got my message. Hmmm, I wonder if he is upset or annoyed with me. Maybe he doesn't know the answer. Now what do I do? I guess I should take my business elsewhere." Most people expect a response, even if it is just an acknowledgement of receipt. If you don't know the answer and have to do more research, just tell the person that you will respond shortly.

- For email communication, consider scheduling a time in your day to focus on answering emails rather than responding to every little ping.[vi] If

vi Kruse, K. "15 Surprising Things Productive People Do Differently." *Forbes*. 20 January 2016. Web. 30 April 2017. https://www.forbes.com/sites/kevinkruse/2016/01/20/15-surprising-things-productive-people-do-differently/#97b59d944b27

you cannot respond to an email right away because it takes thought or research, mark it as unread or flag it so that you won't forget that you didn't respond. Better yet, respond to the person to acknowledge receipt and tell him that you will respond as soon as possible.

- For materials management, consider the acronym OHIO as your new mantra—only handle it once. Whether emails, paper mail, or any communication or task, try to handle it just once. In other words, do something with it the first time you touch it. If you open mail, recycle the junk mail as you are opening it and put any bills or important mail on your desk or wherever you will deal with it. Don't leave mail to pile up and clutter your life. If you use resources and materials to complete a task or project, put them away as soon as you are finished. Don't keep moving them from place to place thinking, "I'll get to it later." Maintaining an organized and efficient workplace will be noticed and help you move upward and onward.[vii]

- Whenever you need an approval or clarification from your boss, peers, etc., say, "I would like your advice and guidance in this matter." This makes the other person feel important. You are not only involving that person in the decision but you are giving him part of the responsibility too.

- When asking something of someone, frame it with the opening words, "Would you kindly …" And of course, always remember those magic words you learned in kindergarten, "please," "thank you," "you're welcome," and "excuse me."

If you feel like you could use some additional coaching on bridging the gap between your college/university earned skills and performing well in the "real world," you can always consider utilizing a program like Roadmap.[viii] Roadmap's unique and proven KNOW PLAN ACT™ Method teaches students to

- know what you need to learn,

- plan how to use that information, and

- act on that plan with confidence.

Roadmap is like SAT prep for career success. It's an online tool and mobile app that teaches students everything they need to know—and do—to successfully transition to life in the real world.

[vii] Kruse, K. "15 Surprising Things Productive People Do Differently." *Forbes*. 20 January 2016. Web. 30 April 2017. https://www.forbes.com/sites/kevinkruse/2016/01/20/15-surprising-things-productive-people-do-differently/#97b59d944b27

[viii] RoadMap. http://theroadmap.com/

8.7: The Take Away

- When crafting your cover letter, résumé, and/or application, submit all documents in full and error free.

- Relate your skills and interests to the job that is posted. Customize your cover letter and résumé for each position. Remember, rarely is there a one-size-fits-all résumé or cover letter.

- All written communication should be error free, should address the recipient formally (Mr., Mrs., Miss, Ms.), and should correctly spell the recipient's name.

- When searching for a job, utilize every possible resource (e.g., major websites that list thousands of jobs, industry-specific websites, websites of targeted companies, recruiting agencies, the career placement center at your college/university). Most career centers will also help graduates, so if you didn't utilize the career center while you were attending, you may still be able to go back and receive help.

- Network, network, network. Attend fairs or events specific to your field. If there is a professional organization for your field, join it. Use networking-oriented sites like LinkedIn.

- Be sure to thank anyone who helped you along the way!

- When you do acquire employment, remember that the workplace is filled with employees who bring years of experience and expertise to their job. Recognize and utilize the strengths of all team players, and remember that it can take time to find your place and feel comfortable as a new employee.

- Utilize all those important social and EQ skills. Sometimes it takes a lot of patience and perseverance to be able to work cooperatively with certain personalities!

- Your first job may not be your lifelong job. Sometimes it takes time to get to the place you want to be, but every job offers learning opportunities that will help you become a better person and employee.

BIBLIOGRAPHY

Andersen, E. (2014, April 7). How Google picks new employees (Hint: It's not about your degree). *Forbes*. Retrieved from https://www.forbes.com/sites/erikaandersen/2014/04/07/how-google-picks-new-employees-hint-its-not-about-your-degree/#5f6ea23625e4

Bozman, R. (Producer), & Dey, T. (Director). (2006). *Failure to Launch* [Motion Picture]. United States: Paramount.

Bradberry, T. (2016, May 18). 8 great tricks for reading people's body language. *Entrepreneur*. Retrieved from https://www.entrepreneur.com/article/275309

The Career Psychologist. (2012, June 3). Tug of war with the anxiety monster. Retrieved from http://www.thecareerpsychologist.com/tug-of-war-with-the-anxiety-monster/

Chew, J. (2016, April 29). Here's how much NFL draft pick Laremy Tunsil lost because of 1 tweet. *Fortune*. Retrieved from http://fortune.com/2016/04/29/laremy-tunsil-tweet-video/

Communication [for English Language Learners]. (n.d.). In *Merriam-Webster Online*. Retrieved from https://www.merriam-webster.com/dictionary/communication

Costas, C. & Mnuchin, S. (Producers), & Meyers, N. (Director). (2015). *The Intern* [Motion Picture]. United States: Warner Brothers.

Dietz, L. (n.d.). Mind states. Retrieved from https://www.dbtselfhelp.com/html/mind_states.html

Dietz, L. (n.d.). Myths about emotions. Retrieved from https://dbtselfhelp.com/html/myths.html

Dintersmith, T., & Wagner, T. (2016, August 31). America desperately needs to redefine 'college and career ready.' *MarketWatch*. Retrieved from http://www.marketwatch.com/story/america-desperately-needs-to-redefine-college-and-career-ready-2016-08-05

Educate to Advance. (2017, June 3). Women—12 tips to ace your job interview. Retrieved from http://www.educatetoadvance.com/women-12-tips-to-ace-your-job-interview/

Ferenstein, G. (2014, April 25). Why Google doesn't care about college degrees, in 5 quotes. *VentureBeat*. Retrieved from https://venturebeat.com/2014/04/25/why-google-doesnt-care-about-college-degrees-in-5-quotes/

Fulghum, R. (1988). *Everything I ever really needed to know I learned in kindergarten*. Evanston, IL: Press of Ward Schori.

Fertig, A. (2015, October 6). 4 communication skills to highlight on your résumé. *U.S. News & World Report*. Retrieved from http://money.usnews.com/money/

blogs/outside-voices-careers/2015/10/06/4-communications-skills-to-high-light-on-your-resume

Fertig, A. (2015, October 27). The 10 best websites to find jobs. *U.S. News & World Report*. Retrieved from http://money.usnews.com/money/blogs/outside-voices-careers/2015/10/27/the-10-best-websites-to-find-jobs

Forbes Coaches Council. (2017, January 24). 11 habits the best networkers have. *Forbes*. Retrieved from https://www.forbes.com/sites/forbescoachescouncil/2017/01/24/11-habits-the-best-networkers-have/#53b9851923a4

Gallo, C. (2017, March 28). Top 7 VCs say these communication skills will set you apart. *Forbes*. Retrieved from https://www.forbes.com/sites/carmine-gallo/2017/03/28/7-top-vcs-say-these-communication-skills-will-set-you-apart/#46a502cb65df

Gausepohl, S. (2016, December 5). Tackling 4 key challenges of the multigenerational workforce. *Business News Daily*. Retrieved from http://www.businessnewsdaily.com/6609-multigenerational-workforce-challenges.html

Grasz, J. (2014, April 10). Overwhelming majority of companies say soft skills are just as important as hard skills, according to a new CareerBuilder survey. *CareerBuilder*. Retrieved from http://www.careerbuilder.com/share/aboutus/pressreleasesdetail.aspx?ed=12/31/2014&id=pr817&sd=4/10/2014

Hayes, S. C., Strosahl, K., & Wilson, K. G. (1999). *Acceptance and commitment therapy: An experiential approach to behavior change*. New York: Guilford Press, p. 109.

Hertzberg, K. (2017, June 2). How to end an email: 9 never-fail sign-offs and 9 to avoid. *Grammarly Blog*. Retrieved from https://www.grammarly.com/blog/how-to-end-an-email/

Kersten, D. (2002, November 15). Today's generations face new communication gaps. *USA Today*. Retrieved from http://usatoday30.usatoday.com/money/job-center/workplace/communication/2002-11-15-communication-gap_x.htm

Kruse, K. (2016, January 20) 15 surprising things productive people do differently. *Forbes*. Retrieved from https://www.forbes.com/sites/kevinkruse/2016/01/20/15-surprising-things-productive-people-do-different-ly/#97b59d944b27

Lythcott-Haims, J. (2016). *How to raise an adult: Break free of the overparenting trap and prepare your kid for success*. New York: Saint Martin's Griffin.

Metta Psychology Group. (2017, January 18). The 4 goals of misbehavior in children. *Metta Psychology Group*. Retrieved from http://www.mettapsych.com/news/2017/1/18/the-4-goals-of-misbehavior-in-children

Mogel, W. (2008). *The blessing of a skinned knee: Using Jewish teachings to raise self-reliant children*. New York: Scribner.

Nathanson, H. (2017, June 5). Harvard rescinds acceptances for at least ten students for obscene memes. *The Harvard Crimson*. Retrieved from http://www.thecrimson.com/article/2017/6/5/2021-offers-rescinded-memes/

Ni, P. (2013, September 2). Ten keys to handling unreasonable & difficult people. *Psychology Today*. Retrieved from https://www.psychologytoday.com/blog/communication-success/201309/ten-keys-handling-unreasonable-difficult-people

Pullman, E. (2013, November 18). Secrets of successful roommate relationships. *The Huffington Post*. Retrieved from http://www.huffingtonpost.com/elizabeth-pietr-zak/secrets-of-successful-roo_b_4278163.html

RoadMap. http://theroadmap.com/

Rochman, B. (2013, February 22). Hover no more: Helicopter parents may breed depression and incompetence in their children. *Time*. Retrieved from http://healthland.time.com/2013/02/22/hover-no-more-helicopter-parents-may-breed-depression-and-incompetence-in-their-children/

Rowe, M. (2017, May 27). The jobs that exist right now don't require massive college debt. *ATTN:*. Retrieved from https://www.facebook.com/attn/videos/1388355794533209/

Satell, G. (2015, February 6). Why communication is today's most important skill. *Forbes*. Retrieved from https://www.forbes.com/sites/gregsatell/2015/02/06/why-communication-is-todays-most-important-skill/#1566640c1100

Self-presentation. (n.d.). In *Babylon Thesaurus*. Retrieved from http://thesaurus.babylon-software.com/self-presentation

Sterner, T. M. (2012). *The practicing mind: Developing focus and discipline in your life*. Novato, CA: New World Library.

Sullivan, J. (2013, May 20). Why you can't get a job ... recruiting explained by the numbers. *ERE Media*. Retrieved from https://www.ere.net/why-you-cant-get-a-job-recruiting-explained-by-the-numbers/

TalentSmart. (2017, May 8). About emotional intelligence. Retrieved from http://www.talentsmart.com/about/emotional-intelligence.php

Youth in Transition Project. (n.d.). Adolescent Autonomy Checklist. Retrieved from http://www.sped.sbcsc.k12.in.us/PDF%20Files/tassessments/Independent%20Living/Adolescent%20Autonomy%20Checklist.pdf

APPENDIX

WHERE TO TURN— ADDITIONAL RESOURCES

In Print

Blanchard, K., & Bowles, S. (1993). *Raving Fans*. New York: William Morrow and Co., Inc.

To learn customer service tips and techniques that can turn customers into raving and spending fans.

Blanchard, K., & Johnson, S. (2015). *The New One-Minute Manager*. New York: William Morrow and Co., Inc.

To help today's future managers succeed more quickly in a rapidly changing world.

Cain, S. (2012). *Quiet: The Power of Introverts in a World That Can't Stop Talking*. New York: Random House.

To understand different personalities you find in the office.

Covey, S. (1989), *The 7 Habits of Highly Effective People*. New York: Free Press.

A non-fiction, self-help book that helps one solve personal and professional problems and helps align one's values with so-called "universal and timeless" principles.

Friedman, D. (2011). *Fundamentally Different*. West Conshohocken, PA: Infinity Publishing.

To understand company culture.

Rath, T. (2007). *StrengthsFinders 2.0*. New York: Gallup Press. A non-fiction book that provides an assessment tool for identifying your strengths, specifically your top 5 talents, and then provides 10 strategies for building on each of your top 5 talents.

Sinek, S. (2009). *Start with Why: How Great Leaders Inspire Everyone to Take Action*. London: Penguin Group

To help people become more innovative, influential, and inspired at work, and in turn inspire their colleagues and customers.

Syed, M. (2015). *Black Box Thinking: Why Most People Never Learn from Their Mistakes—But Some Do.* New York: Penguin Random House.
To better understand how success in any field requires an acknowledgment of failure and a willingness to engage with it because success can happen only when we confront and learn from our mistakes.

On the Web

ACT, Inc.
http://www.act.org/content/act/en/products-and-services/the-act.html

CollegeBoard
https://www.collegeboard.org/

ERE Media
http://www.eremedia.com

Idealist Careers
http://idealistcareers.org/a-quick-guide-to-writing-your-elevator-pitch-with-examples/

Medzilla
www.medzilla.com

Resume-Now
https://www.resume-now.com/builder/rbdesktop/edit-resume.aspx

Roadmap
www.theroadmap.com

On Campus

The Guidance Office (in the high school setting)

The guidance office offers many resources to students. A school counselor can link students to services such as academic support and college, career, and financial aid planning.

Registrar's Office

Provides administrative academic support for current and former students. Questions about registration, courses needed for major and/or minor work, transfer credits, grades, etc. can be answered by the staff in this office.

Orientation or New Student Programs